So I gently offer my hand and ask,
Let me find my talk
So I can teach you about me.

— RITA JOE

Women and Environmental Network in Thailand (WENIT)

WENIT is a network of academics, activists and journalists who are interested in working collaboratively with grassroots women engaged in environmental movements to protect their community's livelihood and who seek their own rights and opportunities to participate at all levels of decision-making on the utilisation and management of their community's natural resources.

The network's main concerns are to intellectually empower and enhance the roles of grassroots women in environmental movements locally and globally, to make challenging and critical contributions to feminist theories for social change, and to influence the public, NGOs and policy-makers to be more sensitised to gender perspectives in environmental issues.

In order to achieve these goals, our work is designed to cover, in depth and breadth, the activities of dialogue, documenting, researching and theorising women's indigenous wisdom, viewpoints and experiences in order to strategically build up the 'body of knowledge' in the needed and promising area of 'Women and Environment'.

The network invites sponsorship from individuals and groups who are interested in financing our work or contributing in some ways towards intellectually advancing and strengthening women's role in the environmental movement for social change.

For more information, please contact
WENIT
535/18 Jarunsanitwong Rd 39
Bangkok 10700
Thailand
Tel/Fax (662) 411-4046

The Daughters of Development

WOMEN AND THE CHANGING ENVIRONMENT

SINITH SITTIRAK

Zed Books
LONDON & NEW YORK

The Daughters of Development
was first published by
Zed Books Ltd, 7 Cynthia Street, London N1 9JF, UK
and Room 400, 175 Fifth Avenue, New York, NY 10010, USA
in 1998

A catalogue record for this book
is available from the British Library

ISBN   Hb 1 85649 587 6
         Pb 1 85649 588 4

Distributed in the USA exclusively by St Martin's Press Inc.,
175 Fifth Avenue, New York, NY 10010, USA.

Contents

Acknowledgements

The act of writing, like that of living, is 'round'. When one approaches the end, one always goes back to rethink the starting point. Although the acknowledgements are always found on the first few pages of any piece of formal writing, it isn't until the work is completed that they are finally written. As I come closer to finishing my major project and going home, I have begun to think about the last day in Bangkok before I had left for Toronto four years ago.

It was on Friday, 7 September 1990 that my mother met with Professor Malee Pruekpongsawalee, the Director of the Women in Development Consortium in Thailand (WIDCIT). WIDCIT was a Canadian International Development Agency (CIDA) joint project between Thammasat and York University. It provided me with a scholarship to come and study in Canada.

On that day, my mother asked the professor many questions, such as 'Will there be someone to pick her up at the airport? Where will she stay? How far is the market? If she is sick, who will take care of her?' and so on. At that moment, I felt embarrassed and whispered to myself '... Mum, why don't you ask some "academic" questions such as "What courses do they offer at the Faculty of Environmental Studies?"'

Four years have passed; my mother is now close to eighty and is becoming senile. She no longer asks many questions. Instead, she asks just a few questions and repeats them many times. The questions she brought up on that day have taken on special meaning for me, and are located in a special corner of my memory. They exemplify 'motherly' concern. I have learned that it is this type of concern that sustains my life in the same way that the earth nurtures her trees.

It will soon be time to go back home and tell my mother that it was a professor and her husband who picked me up at the airport. I have also been living on campus; first, at the 'Assiniboine' Road Graduate Residence and later, at the newly built 'Passy Garden' townhouses. From the window of my room on the third floor, I could see the Stong Pond nearby where the ducks swim and the geese lay down idly under the willow trees. 'Ferlisi', at that time the closest supermarket, was two bus stops away, or about a twenty-minute walk (longer during the winter time). Later, 'Foodland' opened near campus and I was informed that there was a Vietnamese supermarket on Keel Street across from the University. It had a lot of Oriental food which made my life much easier.

Generally, it has been a priceless and unforgettable experience to learn many aspects of Canadian university life during these years, to make many friends from all around the world and be involved in women's and environmental networks. Particularly, at the Faculty of Environmental Studies (FES), I have had an extraordinary opportunity to weave, unweave and reweave many of my personal and political 'threads' into my 'yesterday, today and tomorrow' life fabric. This unique experience would not have been possible if I had not had a solid and rich ground to plant myself in. This was provided by the love, care, respect and understanding of my friends, professors and supporters. First, they include friends from my year (1990), the years after and even from outside FES: Dorothy, Eleanor, Nicola, Marie, Lori, Jamie, Jackie, Sandra, Evan, Julie, Sheila, Connie, Pam, Kevin, Anne Bell, Ann Phillips, Gillian Austin, Luke, Mook, Tippawan, Marianna, Tuanjai etc.; 'company' in the Student Advocacy Service (SAS): Gillian Kranias, Bonita, Suzanne, Marcelo, Eduardo, Mark Lutes, Wiwick, Ramelia, Dawn and Ann Sutherland and...; Executive Members of the Graduate Student Association (GSA) and Board Members of the Centre for Race and Ethnic Relations (whom I had a very challenging opportunity to work with during my last year). Then, there are my 'teachers': dian, Gerda, Deborah, Gerry, Leesa and Mary. Above all, it was the exceptional team of support staff: Alice, Anita, Paula, Pat, Carina, Carol, Bev, Joanne etc. Their 'Hi!' and smiles, their hospitality and 'hands', as well as their thoughtful ideas and spirit have sustained me during my critical moments and inspired me to keep going. I will take their love and spirit with me when I return home. Sincerely, all of them deserve wholehearted thanks from both of us, my mother and me.

Secondly, as my book is entitled *The Daughters of Development*, I must mention all the important men who have helped make these 'daughters' and take care of me during that long 'pregnant' period. First of all, there is my father, who has been a life-long inspiration to me. My father is someone who always spoke soundly in public and showed me how to handle and heal the hard days in life with hope and humour. A man who humbly apologised when he had done wrong. He passed away a long time ago, but his love and spirit still envelop me. Then, there is Pracha who supplied endless magazines, articles and books from Bangkok, and Kanchit who did the same from New York. Chris initiated research on the issue of prostitution in Thailand at Robart's library. From the seventh floor of the Royal Bank Head Office in Toronto, Gilbert provided me with clippings from the *Financial Post* and other relevant economic-related publications. I thank Peter Kohnke for his timely dialogue, contribution and his ecological editing. Peter Penz will always be remembered as a good listener and an introspective, open-minded and ethical adviser.

Finally, my acknowledgements will not be complete unless I extend it to include Indonesian and Thai workers. In my opinion, 'illiterate' is an oppressive word. Therefore, I don't want to claim that I am 'computer illiterate' but I must mention that I wrote my entire book by hand using up to 600 pages of 'Hilroy' paper imported from Indonesia. I also used three dozen 'Niji' stylist and 'Bic' ball point pens made by female factory workers in Thailand who 'clock in and clock off, and in between there is not even time to go to the toilet' (Nelson, 1989: 97).

Just prior to and during my lifetime, the world has changed so dramatically that all of us who are alive today and in the near future cannot escape the decisions that need to be made at this very critical moment. The patriarchal ideology which operates in the form of capitalism and neo-colonialism has brought irreparable damage to our web of life-nature, and made the form and content of human relations to be sexist, classist and racist. There have been many people who try to make things better in many different ways and places. Change is coming along. If I don't see it as much as I wish in my lifetime, I believe my daughter will.

Preface

MARIA MIES

I write this Preface to Sinith Sittirak's book: *The Daughters of Development: Women and the Changing Environment* with a peculiar sense of joy. This joy stems, I think, from a feeling I got while reading her manuscript, that, at last, the tide is turning, that the process of decolonising ourselves, both in the South and in the North, has begun, that the different parts of the world, separated, fragmented and hierarchised by capitalist patriarchy can be reconnected, that the dawn of hope is again arising on the horizon.

This queer feeling of joy and hope stems from the fact that here is a piece of work from a woman from a 'developing' country, who dares to critically appraise the paradigm of 'development' which for at least 30–40 years has been the anchor of hope for most people in Asia, Africa, South America – and that she demolishes this anchor, for many reasons, but particularly because from the perspective of her mother and her motherland, Thailand, development has rather destroyed good life for the majority, above all for women and nature. Sinith Sittirak shows that 'development is plunder', as my friend Claude Alvares from India called it.

I met Sinith Sittirak at the World Congress of Sociology in Bielefeld in July 1994. With Chhaya Datar I had organized a panel for the Research Council 32 (Women in Society) on the theme 'Envisioning the Future: Women and Alternative Development'. Chhaya pointed out to me that there was a most interesting photo exhibition by a Thai woman about what development meant to her mother. Later I met Sinith Sittirak, who gave me her thesis. After I had read it, I noticed that it fitted perfectly into the line of thinking which the twelve panelists – many of them from the South – demonstrated during our session. This consensus was summarised by my friend Claudia von Werlhof: 'The best alternative to development is no development'.

This also summarises the findings of Sinith Sittirak's work. She is one more of those feminist voices from the South who no longer place their hope in the myth of 'catching up' industrial development propagated by the World Bank and GATT, but rather in the preservation and restoration of their mothers' subsistence economy. Looking at development from Sinith's and her mother's perspective at the same time is indeed the most fruitful methodological approach to demystify all the empty and dangerous promises of the growth mania.

This approach reminded me again of our early feminist slogan: 'The personal is political'. Sinith extended it, however, to include both the personal and the sociopolitical history of capitalist patriarchy of the present époque in Thailand. And it prompted me also to reflect again on my own concrete history in its social, economic and political context.

I am writing this from *my* mother's village – a small village 100 km south of Cologne in Germany. This village has also been the target of 'development'. Up to the middle of 1960 most of its inhabitants were still peasants, who partly produced for their own subsistence, partly for the market. Then development set in, with tractors replacing horses, chemical fertiliser replacing cowdung, the use of herbicides and pesticides replacing human labour. All this modernisation was subsidised by credits, particularly the modernisation of dairy-farming, which as a kind of monoculture replaced the old mixed farming system. More and more the money economy penetrated the village, and production for external markets destroyed what still was left of self-provisioning subsistence production. This policy was promoted particularly by the government and the European Union who wanted to 'modernise' agriculture to such an extent that only about 5 per cent of the population should be farmers in Europe. The modernisation of the dairy sector was promoted through the sale of surplus milk powder to India, for example, which then began her 'White Revolution' or 'Operation Flood' in the 1970s. Many small farmers here gave up farming because only the big ones were favoured by this 'development'. Young people left the village because they could earn more money in the city. Young women did not want to marry a farmer any more, because it meant helping with field work, dairying and other farm work. 'A peasant stinks' became a saying in the villages around here. They wanted to be full-time housewives, like urban housewives, and preferred to marry men with a wage or salary. Money does not stink. Gradually the peasants developed a kind of inferiority complex which is similar to the one of colonised people which Sinith Sittirak describes in her work; the more the farmers tried to 'catch-up' with the urbanites, however, the more they felt 'backward'. Some of the men here, who could not find a wife among the local girls, have imported a wife from Thailand or the Philippines.

The new liberalisation and globalisation of the agrarian markets, promoted since the 1990s by the World Bank, GATT and now the World Trade Organisation, have hit my mother's village more drastically. Many more farmers have given up farming; only a handful of the biggest have remained. The small ones cannot compete with the cheap food imports from cheap-labour countries, also from Thailand. But, contrary to some years ago, they are also unable to find alternative employment in industry. So they have to live on the government's dole.* One can see them walk idly around the village, which looks more and more like an urban suburb. The houses are all renovated, the streets are clean, no work, no cows, no children, no noise, except for a few cars now and again. All families have fridges, TVs, cars, washing machines. Everywhere there are empty stables and barns, now useless farm machinery. This is development.

But this development has its price, too. The community has a debt-burden of DM1 million. A magnificent volcanic hill, a landmark for the whole region, was destroyed. Its sand was excavated and used to construct those famous German autobahns. Now there is only a hole, and the money and the few jobs are also gone.

The most recent manifestation of development here is the new garbage policy. Ten years ago the concept of organic 'waste' – kitchen garbage, leaves from garden trees, etc. – did not exist here. 'Waste' was immediately used as either fodder for pigs or hens or as manure. Now modernisation has set in. People have to collect this kitchen garbage and other organic matter which is now called 'big-waste' and this big-waste is now transported to Thuringia in East Germany (about 800 km away from here) where it is being industrially composted. The district authorities consider this the most advanced, developed, progressive way of dealing with the organic waste of erstwhile peasant villagers who did not know waste till some years ago – this is development. But this is capitalist-patriarchal development. A hole in the ground, devastated nature, devastated people. People who live on the land but depend totally on the state and on the money economy and its global reach.

---

* dole = a certain fixed amount of money to unemployed people for rent and food.

Going to mother's village and looking at development from her perspective is really an eye-opening experience. It shows not only the absurdity of the growth mania and the development paradigm, but the whole bluff behind it. It also helps to see the worldwide interconnections from a village in Thailand, for instance, to a village in Germany – connections, which have been made first by capital, but which on the other hand also involve real people who then may begin to understand the big mystification behind the promises of Mr CAPITAL, namely that money can create life. Particularly nowadays, in the period of global restructuring of the world economy, when after the breakdown of 'really existing' socialism in Eastern Europe, Mr CAPITAL appears as the only saviour, the only alternative in 'postmodernism'. It is a most sobering, enlightening, but also exhilarating experience to go back to mother, and mother's village and land, in order to see that life still comes from living and loving people and their loving interaction with Mother Earth and not from money breeding ever more money.

Sinith Sittirak's going back to her mother happened just at the right time, I feel, in a time when, according to the strategists of the world economy, Thailand has just managed to join the club of the NICs, or the East Asian Tigers. A worldview as that expressed and lived by Sinith's mother is certainly not in the line of those Tigers. Because tigers cannot live without hunting for prey. Or, as Saral Sarkar, my Indian husband, put it: 'Everybody wants to be a tiger nowadays. But who will be the goats?'

Sinith's mother knows who the goats are, so does Sinith Sittirak, so do many women and some men in the South and also some women and men in the North. But in the end the goats may not be as helpless as they may appear. Once we have got clarity about the functioning of global capitalist patriarchy, once we have penetrated the smoke screen that the discourse on development, modernisation, and progress has created, it is possible to also find another vision of a better society and economy, a society and economy which do not need to exploit and colonise nature, women, peasants and other people in order to have a good life.

The method of the combination of an inside-out and an outside-in perspective can be a wonderful means to achieve this clarity. Particularly when it is combined with an analysis of concrete everyday life practices and life-histories and their changes due to 'development'. Such analysis carried out in our mothers' villages and from a perspective like the one Sinith Sittirak shows in her work, both in the South and in the North, can lead us also to learn from each other how to overcome the material and non-material trappings of capitalist patriarchy.

Maria Mies
Steffeln, Germany

Foreword

... it is important to recognize that questions of conceptual-isation are questions of power, that is, they are political questions. In this sense, the clarification of conceptual positions is part of the political struggle of feminism (Mies, 1989: 36).

The goal of my study is to integrate and synthesise the components of my area of concentration, that is, the exploration of the conceptual background and concrete conditions of development, women and environment as they are related to, affected by or reflected in each other.

I chose to explore this area because of a concern I have had regarding Thailand's three decades of neo-colonisation and the importation of Western ideology and technology which came with the former's drive to become one of the 'developing' countries, i.e. to pull itself out of 'backwardness' into the forward momentum of global economic progress. Instead of achieving progress, our physical and cultural environments have been destroyed in order to serve the consumerist habits of a few hegemonic interests. Also of concern to me is the fact that this crisis directly affects women the most, as they are the ones who work in close relation to nature, and who are the poorest among the poor. Thai women had originally been maintainers of environmental indigenous knowledge. Many have now become either primary producers whose labour is exploited to produce commodity goods for others, or 'commodities' (i.e. prostitutes*) themselves.

My study utilises a feminist critique by integrating several Thai perspectives to explicate the changing role of Thai women resulting from social, political, economic and environmental changes brought on by development. To bring these changes into relief, I focused on a study of prostitution in Thailand in terms of global militarism and consumerism. Additionally, in order to sharpen that critique, I also incorporated the personal history of my mother and myself to emphasise the changes that have occurred in Thailand as a result of development. I have included these histories in the belief that:

> there is no better point of entry into a critique or a reflection than one's own experience. It is not the end point, but the beginning of an exploration of the relationship between the personal and the social and therefore the political. And this connecting process, which is also a discovery, is the real pedagogic process, the 'science' of social science (Bannerji, 1991: 67).

Six chapters, each sharing the common theme question of 'what does "development" mean to ...?', compose the structure of the book. The first chapter asks the question 'what does development mean to *me*'?; that is, what have I learned about

---

* 'Prostitute' is another example of oppressive language. The more appropriate term which is widely used now is 'sex worker'. However, in this study, I leave it as it is to reflect its research period.

the meaning of development through my own experiences and how has this process of learning taken place? The second part asks: what does development mean to *them*, the male mainstream development theorists? The third part, asking 'what does development mean to *her*?', reflects on the work of two authors who constructed a feminist critique of development. The fourth part critically reflects on the question 'what does development mean to *us*, the prostitutes of Thailand?' The remaining two chapters, five and six, contain the oral, environmental and historical exploration of what development means to 'my mother' as well as returning to my initial question in chapter one, but this time with a renewed and more critical understanding. These two chapters, then, explore an understanding of the meaning of 'development' which goes beyond that of the traditional paradigm of political economy in that it instead recognises the politics of identity and difference. This study is also an attempt to contribute to and join in the process of theory transformation as envisioned and described by Anzaldúa:

What is considered theory in the dominant academic community is not necessarily what counts as theory for women of colour. Theory produces effects that change people and the way they perceive the world. Thus we need *teorias* that will enable us to interpret what happens in the world, that will explain how and why we relate to certain people in specific ways, that will reflect what goes on between inner, outer and peripheral 'I's within a person and between the personal 'I's and the collective 'we' of our ethnic communities.

Theory, then, is a set of knowledges. Some of these knowledges have been kept from us – entry into some professions and academia denied us. Because we are not allowed to enter discourse, because we are often dis-qualified and excluded from it, because what passes for theory these days is forbidden territory for us, it is *vital* that we occupy theorizing space, that we not allow white men and women solely to occupy it. By bringing in our own approaches and methodologies, we transform that theorizing space (1990: xxv).

Finally, the title of the study, *The Daughters of Development: Women and the Changing Environment* refers to my hundred thousand younger and older sisters, who are 'prostitutes', and other women like myself. We are the people who were born and continue to struggle in this era of 'development', although in very different ways.

They call it giving. *We call it self-gratification.*
We call it self-gratification.
They call it give-and-take. *We call it take-and-take.*
We call it take-and-take.
They call it generosity. *We call it conditioning the beggar's mind.*
We call it conditioning the beggar's mind.
Today, to survive the poor can hardly refuse to accept
They say they don't give anymore
Because we are ungrateful
The ungrateful acceptor / *The expecting donor*
They say they don't give anymore because we are ungrateful.
We ponder: Will the donor species survive?

TRINH T. MINH-HA

1

What Does 'Development' Mean to Me?

On 31 July 1990, I received, while living in Bangkok, a letter of welcome sent directly from Toronto:

> I'm pleased to advise you that you have been accepted into a scholarship program provided by the Consortium for the Study of Women's Issues, Institutional Linkage Program (funded by the Canadian International Development Agency).[1]

This particular institutional linkage programme is called 'Women in Development Consortium in Thailand' (WIDCIT). It is a joint project between York University in Canada and universities in Thailand, and one of its primary objectives is *'to cooperate and share ideas and expertise among experts in the field of women and development from governmental and non-governmental agencies and organizations'*.[2]

Today, the issues of 'Women in Development' have become

---

[1] Letter dated 23 July 1990 from John Van Esterik, Ph.D., Thai Studies Project, York University.
[2] Women in Development Consortium in Thailand (WIDCIT) (Bangkok: Thammasat University, 1989, 2.)

increasingly familiar within the Thai context. There are many government and non-government development projects related to women's issues. However, personally speaking, it was the first time that the term 'Women in Development' touched my life directly. Unlike many other women involved in the various development schemes, I did not receive funding for developing projects, such as weaving, chicken raising or making artificial flowers; instead, funding came in the form of a scholarship provided by a project with the intent '*to utilise social sciences and related fields to guide women's development in Thailand* '.[3]

It was a moment of happiness and hopefulness. Like many other students in the so-called 'Third World' countries, to receive a scholarship to study abroad in North America, Europe or even Japan, is a sign or milestone of success in one's life. At that crucial moment, I did not question why the Canadian government was so concerned with the issues that concerned Thai women. *Why do Thai Women need to be 'developed'? (read – Does this mean that Canadian women have already been developed?)*

Additionally, I would not have expected that two months, later, after arriving in this country and attending Professor dian marino's class, 'Media, Culture and Nature', so many burning questions on development would be directed toward me by my classmates. 'What does development mean to you, Sinith?' As the only 'non-Canadian' student in class from a so-called Third World or developing country, it seemed that I was expected to be able to answer all questions on development issues.

'What does development really mean to me?' Looking back at my learning experiences with this problematic term, I am surprised to find that this is one critical academic issue I do not know much about (though I do come from a so-called

[3] Ibid.

'developing country'). I have been very curious since I was young. I used to ask many questions about politics and equal opportunity, such as why are there rich and poor, and why do we have ghettos and prostitution. Surprisingly, I have rarely questioned the concept of 'development', nor have I related it to questions of inequity and injustice in an effort to arrive at a more comprehensive picture. Intuitively, I noticed that there was something wrong with many of the government's development projects, although conceptually I did not pay much attention to the 'larger picture' that sustained them. Influenced by aspects of Marxism (and Maoism), I found that whenever I attempted to analyse social problems, all the sins were easily placed onto more blatant manifestations of the American Imperialist, which included 'his servant dogs' – i.e. the ruling class – rather than to a more subtle form of it.

'What does development really mean to me?' I asked myself. As my previous training was in the field of history, I have difficulty answering any questions without initially referring to a particular historical period. As far as I am able to tell, the term 'development' is fairly new in the Thai context. It seems to have been brought over to Thailand during the late 1950s and early 1960s, with the introduction of large-scale construction of hydro-electric dams, major highway routes and monocultural plantations for export. However, thirty years later, what the Thais have received from development is deforestation, polluted rivers and large numbers of poor and prostitutes. For me, tracing back along this trail of development in Thailand gave me a much clearer picture of *neo-colonisation*.

Surprisingly, I found that the term 'development' had varied over the course of the last 30–40 years. For example, in the late 1950s and 1960s, anti-communist propaganda became the primary vehicle through which the rhetoric of development was disseminated; that is, 'development' understood as the functioning ideology and practice of pro-American

3

Imperialism and through which the imposition of Western ideology and technology and the suppression of traditional knowledge took on a concrete form. Since the late 1970s, when the propaganda of anti-communism had become less effective due to the changing character of global politics, the ideology of 'development' was repackaged into the more politically-neutral language of tourism, agri-business and labour-intensive industrialisation for export. The hope was to achieve the status of one of the 'Newly Industrializing Countries' (NICs) of Asia.

However, living in Canada has taught me to look not only from the outside in, but from the inside out. To be here has given me the opportunity to experience another way of life. Almost every day I receive flyers from Canadian Tire, Zellers, Shopper's Drug Mart, Consumer's Distributing and Eaton's. There are 'sales' seven days a week, every week of the month. Why is there so much in one place and so little in other parts of the world? (Is this the reason why some countries are 'underdeveloped', because others are 'overdeveloped?'). Questions like these persuade me to reconsider the purpose of 'development': that is, the ideology of development hides its own real purpose which is to encourage and maintain the existence of consumerism.

Neo-colonisation and consumerism – these are the first two critical meanings of 'development' that I had discovered after having started my first academic term at a Canadian university as a Third World student funded by a First World development agency. It was the Fall of 1990 ... the leaves changed colour day-by-day as I changed my way of thinking, viewing the world and answering questions night-by-night. At that time I did not know that my understanding of the meaning of the term 'development' was totally different from what it meant to 'them.'

'The government says that it is bringing us progress and development.... For us, their so-called progress means only starvation, dependence, the destruction of our culture and demoralisation of our people.'

'The government says it is creating jobs for our people. But those jobs will disappear along with the forest. In 10 years, the jobs will be gone; and the forest which has sustained us for thousands of years will be gone with them. '

'My father, my grandfather did not have to ask the government for jobs. They were never unemployed. They lived from the land and from the forest [and] we were never hungry or in need.'

ANDERSON MUTANG URUD,
A KELABIT FROM SARAWAK IN MALAYSIA.

2

What Does 'Development' Mean to *Them*?

When I was in Bangkok, I was afraid when I heard about how long and cold winters in Canada are. As it is sunny and bright almost everyday in Thailand, some of my friends even teased me about 'having fun living in a refrigerator!' However, when my first winter came, it was such a pleasant and unforgettable one. I saw my first snow on 2 December 1990. After it was over, I ran to a neighbouring playground to throw snowballs, make a snowman and take pictures of my friends. The winter term started a month later. My plan of study had been revised, focusing more on critiquing of the development concept as it relates to issues on women and environment.

In order to build up the ground work in this area, I enrolled in the courses, 'Basic Needs: Philosophy, Economics and Politics' and 'Women and Development'. While Basic Needs provided me with a basic critical perspective on the philosophical, cultural and political-economic aspects of 'development', Women and Development helped deepen my understanding of the concept of development from a feminist perspective. Since Basic Needs provided access to additional literature on the concept of development, I would now like to share some parts of it here.

To begin, according to Streeten, historically, the discourse on development appears to have had its start in the 1950s when Sir Arthur Lewis and others proposed the 'employment model' as a means to speed up economic growth in an effort to remove mass deprivation, 'a concern that has always been at the heart of development' (Streeten *et al.*, 1981: 9). Since then,

[t]heorists and practitioners of development have written and laboured in universities, government agencies, and international institutions. International conferences have been held, billions have been spent on foreign aid, and thousands of experts now earn their living from development (Wilber and Jameson, 1988: 3).

The main theme of development discourse focused on the causes of deprivation and the approaches and strategies to alleviate it. However, this did not necessarily lead to a consensually accepted understanding as 'this prolonged preoccupation has not resulted in a generally accepted explanation of the process of development' (ibid). Both Wilber and Jameson, in their thorough inquiry based on a number of theories, researches and debates, have concluded that 'there are two main categories of treatments of development, one we will term "orthodox" and the other "political economy"' (ibid).

Let's explore each treatment in brief. Generally, the *orthodox* school does not see deprivation as the result of unequal power between classes, regions or nations, but as resulting from deficiencies in economic functioning. For instance, one key concept and strategy of this school emphasises economic growth as a way to eradicate poverty, which in turn can be further subcategorised into two general developmental streams: growth first – trickle down later, and growth with equity.

The first stream can be broadly represented by three theories or models. For example, one theory, outlined by Arthur Lewis in his popular book, *The Theory of Economic*

Growth, explains the cause of deprivation as the result of unemployment. Therefore, he perceives that modern industries will be the key to resolving the issue of poverty by generating jobs for the poor in an effort to overcome unemployment. As he predicts in his influential 'employment model':

> subsistence farmers and landless labourers would move from the countryside to the higher income, urban, modern industries. This move would increase inequality in the early stages (as long as rural inequalities were not substantially greater than urban inequalities), but when more than a critical number of rural poor had been absorbed in modern industry, the golden age would be ushered in, when growth is married to greater equality (Streeten *et al.*, 1981: 11).

Another theory is the so-called Simon Kuznets' curve which emphasises and therefore reinforces the necessity of income inequality as a fundamental prerequisite for economic growth which will only later trickle down to the poor:

> [i]n the early stages of development, as income per head increases, inequality tends to grow, and this may mean that absolute poverty for some groups also increases. But eventually the turning point, the bottom of the U curve, is reached, after which growing income is accompanied by greater equality and, of course, reduced poverty (ibid: 10).

Lastly, what has strongly dominated not only academic thought but also political action for a number of decades is W.W. Rostow's stages-of-growth model in which he offers a historical illustration of his vision of the development process:

> [i]t is possible to identify all societies, in their economic dimensions, as lying within one of five categories: the traditional society, the pre-conditions for take-off, the take-off, the drive to maturity, and the age of high mass

consumption (quoted in Charoensin-o-larn, 1988: 26).

Rostow's model is widely known as the 'catching up' theory as it uses Western countries as a universal standard which assumes that:

> present day countries correspond to the 'traditional society' stage or, at best, the 'preconditions' stage in the Western developed countries. That is, the present-day developed countries were once underdeveloped and all countries move through all these stages (Wilber and Jameson, 1988: 7–8).

In particular, societies in this historical process of development are characterised as moving 'toward ever greater availability of goods and services for their citizens' (ibid: 7). Therefore, for each nation-state, 'progress', as the fruits of development, can be measured by taking into account the average growth in per capita income of the whole population; or, in summary, development means 'growth in per capita GNP' (ibid: 11).

Theoretically, according to all three development proponents, in order to bring about this kind of development, there is no better mechanism than to do nothing, to leave things alone or in a state of 'laissez-faire'. This means that through the automatic mechanism of free choices and exchanges in the market, scarcity will be replaced by abundant output in which production efficiency is ensured by the competitive forces. Besides the laissez-faire approach, the 'planning approach' and 'modernisation theory' have also been developed from the orthodox paradigm in an effort to address so-called 'underdevelopment' or 'anti-development' conditions. Orthodox theorists have assumed that development will effectively take place in an 'unfettered' process of laissez-faire. Therefore, if there is any obstruction or delay in the development process, it is not due to the inadequacies of the theory but to the interfering factors originating in these poor countries, such as the inefficiencies of the market system resulting from certain government regulations, indigenous local culture and/or non-rational behaviour which helps maintain traditional economic style and retard modern development. At this point, planning economists propose that the government has a crucial role to play in modernising the country and planning the economy:

> [the] government must intervene in the economy to offset the anti-development impact of the two types of obstacles to development. On the side of non-rational behaviour, the government can attempt to convince its citizens of the need for 'modernisation' while at the same time, substituting its own entrepreneurial ability and knowledge to fill that vacuum. On the side of markets, the government can again offset the difficulties through economic planning. By developing a coherent overview of the economy and by forcing this on the actors in the economy through the various means at its disposal, the orthodox result of growth in income can be attained (ibid: 9).

However, in reality the growth-oriented approach doesn't work out as its rhetoric would have us believe. Many development plans and projects around the world have proved to be disappointing failures as testified by Mahbub ul Hag, a Pakistani economist:

> [i]n country after country, economic growth is being accompanied by rising disparities, in personal as well as in regional incomes. In country after country, the masses are complaining that development has not touched their ordinary lives. Very often, economic growth has meant very little social justice. It has been accompanied by rising unemployment, worsening social services and increasing absolute and relative poverty (quoted in Griffin, 1989: 166).

Why has the increase in the growth rate of GNP taken place without resolving issues of massive unemployment, income distribution and stagnation? There are at least three main reasons that need to be considered in order to explain these failures.

First, the trickle-down theory, which assumes the re-distribution of income from the wealthy élite to the rest of society, is very idealistic because both the élite's economic and political power have accumulated and been secured through this unjust growth. Their political power is then used to maintain or crystallise their interest and status and to oppose any attempt to redistribute their accumulated wealth to the poor. Moreover, income is often spent on those goods, such as a university education, luxury mansions or vacations, which cannot be readily shared with the poor. Secondly, the degree of unemployment is far greater than had been originally estimated. Todaro, quoted by Wilber and Jameson, has shown that 'for every job opening up in the cities, three people migrate from rural areas looking for jobs. Thus, for every job created, two people are attracted who end up unemployed' (1988: 12). Moreover, research undertaken by the International Labour Organisation (ILO) Employment Mission has shown that the root problem was not unemployment but poverty or low-productivity employment. The poor in developing countries work extremely hard for long hours, especially women, who 'perform hard tasks without being counted as members of the labour force because their production is not sold for cash' (Streeten *et al.*, 1981: 13). Thirdly, the growth model is contradictory in that it has been developed in such a way that its effect is that of consuming its own organs. The success of their industrialisation process, for example, has been fed by agricultural surpluses at the expense of both natural resources and people's livelihoods. This is then in contradiction with their claim that development will leave people better off economically, as the agricultural sector itself has become neglected and remains too exhausted even to provide for the basic food needs of the poorer farmers and their families.

To correct the failures arising from the inadequacies of the 'growth now, trickle-down later' model, many orthodox theorists perceive an urgent need to modify their development vision to include 'a concern for channelling the benefits of growth to the poorest' (Wilber and Jameson, 1988: 11). That is 'growth with equity', a newly adopted approach which covers some seven fundamental strategies: employment generation, the redirecting of investment, the meeting of basic needs, human resource development, agriculture-first development, integrated rural development and the New International Economic Order.

Of these seven strategies, the two more predominant ones are the 'New International Economic Order' and 'meeting basic needs'. The former calls for 'a major restructuring of those international institutions – the international monetary system, tariffs, multinational corporations, etc. – that at present result in discrimination against the poor countries' (ibid: 13). The latter suggests that 'the goal or target of development should be to meet the basic needs of all people everywhere – food, water, clothing, shelter, medical care, education and participation in decision making' (ibid).

Next, let's explore the *political economy* paradigm. What makes it different from the previous orthodox paradigm? Wilber and Jameson have clearly argued that while the orthodox theorists have focused their attention on economic growth as the goal and measure of progress, the 'political economists are more concerned with the *nature of the process* by which economic growth is achieved' (ibid: 14). The key characteristic of this school can be readily identified by applying Paulo Freire's question regarding the educational process to the development process: 'Are people (or classes) and nations *objects* of development under someone else's control or are they *subjects* of development, in control of their own destiny?' (ibid). As Wilber and Jameson explain:

> traditional economists look on people's values as means.
> Since the goal is growth, if people's values have to change
> in order to get growth, their society must effect that change.
> But for political economists, one goal is to enhance people's
> core values. Development or growth is desirable only if it is
> consistent with people's deepest values (ibid).

The two different approaches of inquiring into why the process of development in some regions or countries has progressed more than in others have evolved from two major schools of thought within this broader paradigm. First, there are the Marxists who believe that the present causes of deprivation are rooted in the capitalist system whereby exploitation and powerlessness are built right into the basic relationship between capitalists and workers.

However, there are different interpretations as to the relationship between politics and economics in the Marxist school of thought. As Staniland summarises:

> [first, there is an instrumentalist tradition, which is heavily
> economistic but in Marxological terms undeniably authen-
> tic. Second, there is a structuralist tradition…, distinguished
> by its assertion that the state can and sometimes must act
> independently of the class whose economic power it is
> structurally bound to preserve. Third, there is a school that
> emphasises the central role of cultural processes in legiti-
> mising class power and the central role of the state in gen-
> erating the symbols of hegemony which gives authority and
> credibility to class power (1985: 167).

While the Marxists focused on a dynamic internal class structure as the key to understanding the control of economic surplus, the dependency theorists were concerned with the connection between the internal class structure within and external relationships between nations. This means that

14

capitalists in developed countries are able to maintain their wealth and power because of the supply of cheap resources and labour from developing countries that they have access to as a result of the cooperation between Multinational Corporations (MNCs) and local capitalists.

In sum, Wilber and Jameson have succinctly summarised the principal focus of this school of thought in the following way:

> [t]he simplest way to understand the meaning of underdevelopment in dependency theory is to see it as a process whereby an underdeveloped country, characterised by subsistence agriculture and domestic production, progressively becomes integrated as dependency into the world market through trade or investment. Its production becomes geared to the demands of the world market and particularly of the developed countries, with a consequent lack of integration between the parts of the domestic economy. Thus, both agriculture and industry become export oriented (1988: 19).

However, no discourse on development can be complete without having touched upon a new stream of thought, that is, *development alternatives*, which emerged as a challenge to mainstream thinking in the 1970s. This development approach is described by Denis Goulet as 'liberation'. Quoting his mentor, Gustavo Gutierrez, a Peruvian theologian and social activist, Goulet states that:

> it is better to speak of liberation, a term which directly suggests domination, vulnerability in the face of world market forces, weak bargaining positions, the need for basic social chances domestically and for freer foreign policies (1979: 381).

In addition, Verhelst has brought culture, the forgotten dimension in development discourse, to the forefront. He argues for the recognition of 'the enduring quality of indigenous cultures and discovering their vitality' (1990: 22) in the belief that:

> it must be understood that development is not the only reference for what is desirable. Since there are many cultures, there are also many ways of envisaging life, happiness and unhappiness. Many ways, also, of perceiving progress (ibid: 63).

Many unique indigenous cultures have gradually been degraded by 'models of social change based on consumption, competition, acquisition and on the manipulation of human aspirations' (ibid: 19). Verhelst discusses the Eurocentric process of development and Western conscientisation which has brought irredeemable damage to the Third World, stripping people of their identity, undermining their capacity for self-determination and pushing them into a dependency situation. As he argues:

> [t]he real tragedy of 'underdevelopment' is that of the gradual destruction of consciousness, by forcing people into dependency. The resulting disintegration or destructuration of society may go as far as an internalised negation of one's self and thus of one's real vitality (ibid: 61).

Finally, Wilber and Jameson argue that besides economics, politics or culture, historical conditions should be considered. They refer to it as 'convoluted history' which is based on Marquez's idea that '… there is no simple historical march of progress. There are no general paths to development just as there is no general definition of development. Each people must write its own history' (1988: 24). Moreover, in order to avoid tragedies like those which occurred in Chile and Cambodia, where changes that took place were led by élites rather than a broad based movement, a new level of analysis is needed:

[d]evelopment should be a struggle to create criteria, goals and means for self-liberation from misery, inequality, and dependency in all forms. Crucially, it should be the process a people choose, which heals them from historical trauma, and enables them to achieve a newness on their own terms (ibid: 25).

After having gone through this development literature review, I have come to the same conclusion as Wilber and Jameson, in that development economists are somewhat like misguided diagnosticians. To make their point they cite from *War and Peace* by Tolstoy:

[d]octors came to see Natasha, both separately and in consultation. They said a great deal in French, German and Latin. They criticised one another, and prescribed the most diverse remedies for all the diseases they were familiar with. But it never occurred to one of them to the simple reflection that they could not understand the disease from which Natasha was suffering, as no single disease can be fully understood in a living person; for every living person has his complaints unknown to medicine – not a disease of the lungs, of the kidneys, of the skin, of the heart, and so on, as described in medical books, but a disease that consists of one out of the innumerable combinations of ailments of these organs (ibid: 24–25).

The above metaphor can be applied to the development process since deprivation in each particular continent or nation is caused by different kinds of 'diseases' occurring at specific points in time. How can the 'Western' doctors of development claim to be the only ones who can 'examine' and explain the symptoms? What is more, if 'the best model of development is the one that any society forges for itself on the anvil of its own specific conditions' (Goulet, quoted in Wilber and Jameson, 1988: 24), how can it be given the same general diagnosis and the same prescription of medication and treatment?

Above all, I believe a more promising direction for development could be taken, if the tables were turned so that the so-called silenced 'patients' could diagnose their own symptoms using their own methodologies and language. At the moment, it might not be surprising to find that the ones who create and spread (and re-create and re-spread) all the 'diseases' are the doctors, i.e. development experts, themselves or at least the societies they metaphorically represent.

Feminist consciousness-raising has not significantly pushed women in the direction of revolutionary policies. For the most part, it has not helped women understand capitalism: how it works, as a system that exploits female labour and its inter-connections with sexist oppression. It has not urged women to learn about different political systems .... or encouraged women to invent and envision new political systems. It has not attacked materialism and our society's addiction to over-consumption. It has not shown women how we benefit from the exploitation and oppression of women and men globally or shown us ways to oppose imperialism. Most importantly, it has not continually confronted women with the understanding that the feminist movement to end sexist oppression can be successful only if we are committed to revolution, to the establishment of a new social order.

bell hooks

3

What Does 'Development' Mean to *Her*?

If anyone were to ask me what I remember most about the courses I had taken at the Faculty of Environmental Studies (FES), it would be difficult to give an adequate answer. However, academically I can say that my most unique learning experience was in Professor dian merino's courses, 'Media, Culture and Nature' and 'Critical Education for Social Change'. In both of these courses, merino emphasised 'critical' thinking in terms of a 'structured criticism'. For example, after each session she would ask her students to reflect on their learning experiences in class by answering some of the following questions: *What is in the lecture, assigned articles or group discussion that connects with your experience? What is missing? Who is missing? Why is it missing?*

In applying a structured criticism, I have come to the conclusion that the literature on development discussed in the previous chapter is not only a 'main' but also a 'male' stream approach to development. What is missing, then, is a feminist perspective on development. Why is it missing? In this chapter, I will attempt to answer that question by exploring what development means to 'her'. In particular, I will discuss the analysis by Vandana Shiva and Maria Mies, both of whom apply feminist perspectives in their critique of development.

In her book, *Staying Alive*, an effort resulting from her involvement with women's struggles in India over the past decade, Vandana Shiva emphatically states, in her ecological testimony, that:

> [t]he earth is rapidly dying: her forests are dying, her soils are dying, her waters are dying, her air is dying. Tropical forests, the creators of the world's climate, the cradle of the world's vegetational wealth, are being bull-dozed, burnt, ruined or submerged. In 1950, just over 100 million hectares of forests had been cleared – by 1975, this figure has more than doubled.
>
> Forests are the matrix of rivers and water sources, and their destruction in tropical regions amounts to the desiccation and desertification of land. Every year 12 million hectares of land deteriorate into deserts and are unable to support vegetation or produce food.... Desertification in Sahel in Africa has already killed millions of people and animals. Globally, some 456 million people today are starving or malnourished because of the desertification of croplands (1990: xv–xvi).

Witnessing the alarming rate of global ecological destruction resulting from development undertaken in the name of Western progress, the Indian philosopher argues that 'there must be something wrong with a concept of progress that threatens survival itself' (ibid: xvi). It is impossible for her to accept the explanation that the cause of deprivation is merely a technical problem resulting from deficiencies in economic functioning. Instead, poverty, for Shiva, is a crisis rooted in the continued exploitation and degradation of the natural environment, and politico-socio-economic practices that exacerbate the marginalisation of women, resulting from and sustained by the current process of colonisation necessary for the unfettered growth of industrial capitalism. The latter is, in turn, nurtured by 'a vision of bringing all natural resources into the market economy of commodity production' (ibid: 9). As she argues,

> [t]he poverty crisis of the South arises from the growing scarcity of water, food, fodder and fuel, associated with increasing maldevelopment and ecological destruction.
> … development projects appropriated or destroyed the natural resource base for the production of sustenance and survival. It destroyed women's productivity both by removing land, water and forests from their management and control, as well as through the ecological destruction of soil, water and vegetation systems so that nature's productivity and renewability were impaired (ibid: 5, 3).

Shiva's insightful ecological critique and gender analysis regarding the concept of development has enabled her work to explain more thoughtfully than traditional 'male' stream development theories the historical and conceptual connections between development, colonisation, capitalism, ecological degradation and the subjugation of Third World women, especially as they are related to, affected by and reflected in each other. As she points out,

> '[d]evelopment' was to have been a post-colonial project, a choice for accepting a model of progress in which the entire world remade itself on the model of the colonising modern west, without having to undergo the subjugation and exploitation that colonialism entailed. The assumption was that western style progress was possible for all. Development, as the improved well-being of all, was thus equated

with the westernisation of economic categories – of needs, of productivity, of growth (ibid: 1).

In addition, Shiva, quoting Rosa Luxemburg, argues that historically the concept of development was originally rooted in the early industrial development era of western Europe. At that time, the two fundamental factors that had contributed most to the growth of industrial capitalism were the occupation of other lands by the colonial powers and the collapse of the indigenous economy:

> ...colonialism is a constant necessary condition for capitalist growth: without colonies, capital accumulation would grind to a halt. 'Development' as capital accumulation and the commercialisation of the economy for the generation of 'surplus' and profits thus involved the reproduction not merely of a particular form of creation of wealth, but also of the associated creation of poverty and dispossession. A replication of economic development based on commercialisation of resource use for commodity production in the newly independent countries created the internal colonies (ibid: 1–2).

In the present neo-colonial era, the process of commodity production has been transferred from the centre of colonial power to its periphery on the assumption that this would eradicate poverty through the creation of employment, by increasing affluence associated with the creation of goods and services. However, because the organizing principle of early and modern industrialisation is based on the concept of unfettered utilisation of natural resources necessary for the maximisation of profit and capital accumulation, Shiva argues that not only are the promises of the golden age unrealisable but it would also create crisis in every aspect of life and society. Economically, the conversion from a nature economy, to satisfy basic needs, to a market economy is a shift toward the use of market mechanisms that manipulate nature and human needs in an effort to condition and manage a market environment necessary for maximising capital accumulation and profit. This means that people lose control of their decision-making power over the uses of the local natural resources which had previously been determined by local collective effort based on the consideration of social and environmental needs. Moreover, since these natural resources are the basis for both a traditional economy and women's sustaining economy, the conversion generates the condition for local scarcity as 'resources which supported their survival [are] absorbed into the market economy while they themselves [are] excluded and displaced by it' (ibid: 13).

Politically, a situation of unequal access to natural resources between the privileged and non-privileged groups of society readily creates political unrest both locally and globally. Because the poor have been excluded from the benefits of using their own local natural resources and 'have no purchasing power to register their demands on the goods and services provided by the modern production system' (ibid), they are also the ones who, both directly and indirectly, bear the greatest costs resulting from the degradation of local resource. Ecologically, the energy intensive production processes of the market economy have created severe environmental crises. This results not only from the heavy and uncontrolled demand for raw materials which exceeds the regenerative capacity of the ecosystem but also from the polluting of the air, water and soil which rapidly break down our life support systems.

The observation that contemporary development activities cause ecological instability and promotes and/or intensifies women's subjugation has undermined the claim made by mainstream development theorists that development is 'neutral' in terms of race, class and gender and suggests rather that this is 'the latest and the most brutal expression of a patriarchal ideology' (ibid: xvi). This ideology, rooted deeply in Western history, is not only the basis for the current acts of

> violence to nature, which seems intrinsic to the dominant development model, [but] is also associated with violence to women who depend on nature for drawing sustenance for themselves, their families, their societies. This violence against nature and women is built into the very mode of perceiving both, and forms the basis of the current development paradigm (ibid).

What is more, the concept of development, and its dependence on a particular theory of progress, is neither an isolated nor an accidentally embedded phenomenon in Western thought, but is rather intrinsically related to the advent of modern science:

> [t]he Age of Enlightenment, and the theory of progress to which it gave rise, was centred on the sacredness of two categories: modern scientific knowledge and economic development.
>
> The rise of patriarchal science of nature took place in Europe during the fifteenth and seventeenth centuries as the scientific revolution. During the same period, the closely related industrial revolution laid the foundations of a patriarchal mode of economic development in industrial capitalism. Contemporary science and development conserve the ideological roots and biases of the scientific and industrial revolution even as they unfold into new areas of activity and new domains of subjugation.
>
> The scientific revolution in Europe transformed nature from *terra mater* into a machine and a source of raw material.... Industrialism created a limitless appetite for resource exploitation, and modern science provided the

ethical and cognitive licence to make such exploitation possible, acceptable – and desirable. The new relationship of man's domination and mastery over nature was thus also associated with new patterns of domination and mastery over women, and their exclusion from participation as *partners* in both science and development (ibid: xiv, xvii).

As modern patriarchal science and development can recognise only 'profits' and not life, it needs to construct a number of 'mystifications' to justify its purposes and processes as well as maintain its dominance. For example, 'poverty' is redefined and understood within the terms of a Western standard of material wealth. Any living condition outside this standard is regarded as a 'lack' which needs to be resolved by purchasing goods and services provided by the modern production system. People are seen to be poor 'if they live in self-built housing made from natural materials like bamboo and mud rather than cement houses. They are seen as poor if they wear handmade garments of natural fibre rather than synthetics' (ibid: 10). At this point, Shiva, quoting an African writer, R. Bahro, states that:

> [i]t is useful to separate a cultural conception of subsistence living as poverty from the material experience of poverty that is a result of dispossession and deprivation. Culturally perceived poverty need not be real material poverty: subsistence economies which satisfy basic needs through self-provisioning are not poor in the sense of being deprived (ibid).

The author then uses this claim to support her argument that development ideology has to depict them as living in conditions of poverty because these people 'do not participate overwhelmingly in the market economy, and do not consume commodities produced for and distributed through the market *even though they might be satisfying those needs through self-provisioning mechanisms'* (ibid).

Her argument reminds me of one of the mainstream theories discussed earlier, that is, the 'theory of underdevelopment', according to which development is an automatic and technically determined process: if it has not occurred as expected, there must be obstructing factors originating in these developing countries that need to be 'corrected'. To reiterate, this theory presupposes that:

> [o]ne obstacle to growth may be nonrational behavior, that is, nonmaximizing behavior. Because of cultural dualism, lack of achievement, or other social/cultural/psychological constraints, people tend to behave in ways that perpetuate traditional forms of economy, and thus retard development. Another is the obstacle to the free working of markets created by government regulation and participation in the economy and by the imperfections of markets caused by the low level of development (Wilber and Jameson, 1988: 8).

As a result, mainstream development theories make both implicit and explicit assumptions that need to be demystified and critiqued. For example, one such assumption is that environmentally sound indigenous technologies are regarded as 'backward' or 'unproductive' and 'regeneration of life' is referred to as 'passivity'. Above all, 'destruction' is viewed as 'production' on the assumption that:

> 'production' takes place only when mediated by technologies for commodity production, even when such technologies destroy life. A stable and clean river is not a productive resource in this view: it needs to be 'developed' with dams in order to become so. Women sharing the river as a commons to satisfy the water needs of their families and society are not involved in productive labour: when

substituted by the engineering man, water management and water use become productive activities (Shiva, 1990: 4).

For a number of years, Indian women have taken on a committed and crucial role by being in the forefront of ecological struggles to protect their forests, land and water. By doing so, they have challenged the most fundamental aspects of the Western patriarchal concept of economic development, that is, that production is not a process of profit maximisation and capital accumulation but rather a productivity of sustenance and needs satisfaction. Moreover, the suffering and insights of these people whose lives are still productive of and responsive to nature have revealed and reinforced for us that the monocultural path of progress is destructive and that rather a healthy productivity is dependent upon the diversity intrinsic to the web of life. For example, while 'nature' is conceptualised in Western thinking as an object to be exploited for profit, Indian philosophy values her as 'Prakriti', the living force that supports life:

[t]he everyday struggles of women for the protection of nature take place in the cognitive and ethical context of the categories of the ancient Indian world-view in which nature is Prakriti, a living and creative process, the feminine principle from which all life arises (ibid: xviii).

In conclusion, what Shiva offers as an alternative to traditional development theories is a historical ground-breaking critique developed from Third World women's wisdom, experience and perspectives. That is, Shiva brings the suppressed views of marginalised rural Indian women to the centre and delivers their message that:

... it is now imperative to recover the feminine principle as the basis for development which conserves and is ecological. Feminism as ecology, and ecology as the rival of

Prakriti, the source of life, becomes the decentred powers of political and economic transformation and restructuring (ibid: 7).[1]

However, on the other hand, even though her analysis is understood as a 'breakthrough' in development discourse, there are still many critical points that need to be discussed. For example, Rajni Kothari, another Indian scholar, has convincingly argued that:

[t]here are places where I do not necessarily agree with the author, e.g. with her often explicit and often implied equivalence between women and nature, as if all women are by definition conservationist, life-enhancing and equity-seeking. Although she is aware of the problem, she is not sufficiently discriminating between urban – and urbanised – women devoured by consumerist ethics, and rural and tribal women whose identity with both nature and the human community is so organic and authentic (ibid: ix–x).

Moreover, Kothari helps fill in the missing pieces in Shiva's work by clarifying that:

[i]t is not women alone who are involved in these struggles; that [would] be a gross exaggeration and exaggerating a process only distorts it (in both conceptualising the process and acting it out). It is rather that both as victims of modern

---

[1] To come across a non-Western concept such as the Hindu Prakriti is an eye-opener for me, a Buddhist Thai. It inspires me to think of Buddhist ideology, i.e. how Buddhism perceives and explains the concept of 'nature', in addition to what differences and similarities it shares with Prakriti. To critically rethink Buddhism's uniqueness inspires me to explore further. It also seems to suggest that Prakriti belongs to Hinduism and cannot speak for other non-Western ideologies (i.e. Buddhism).

technological development and the scientific paradigm from which such development derives its *raison d'être*, and as possible deliverers (and liberators) from it, women are more central than men – at any rate such women as still cherish and nurture the feminine principle (not all of them do). They also seem better equipped for opening up new civic spaces as part of both preserving and rebuilding communities. In sum, femininity and ecology on the one hand and femininity and ethnicity on the other are natural allies, mutually synergizing and often found in practice to be synonymous. They are all part of the larger struggle for *endogeneity* in a world threatened by the homogenizing thrust of modernity (ibid: x–xi).

Kothari also raises the issue of class which should have been included in Shiva's discussion. However, what both Indian thinkers rarely touch upon is the ideology of Indian patriarchy prior to the colonisation period. There is no doubt that western patriarchy in the name of science and development has brought irredeemable damage to India in all aspects of life. However, for a number of centuries prior to the colonialists' arrival, the ideology of ancient Indian patriarchy had played a crucial role in oppressing both Indian men and women. This is something that needs to be critiqued in parallel with the critique of Western patriarchy.

As I discussed earlier in chapter two, a more promising direction for development would occur 'if the tables were turned so that the so-called silenced "patients" could diagnose their own symptoms using their own methodologies and language'. In this regard, Shiva and other rural Indian women have, by eloquently turning the table and showing us a powerfully different perspective, participated in the historical revolutionary process of 'returning the gaze' by reconstructing and thereby demystifying the centre's or development experts' own assumed privilege, which cannot be completed without also retrieving the capacity for generating local knowledges.

In response to and in reinforcement of Shiva's and other Indian women's testimony regarding resource depletion in Third World countries,[2] Maria Mies, a leading urban First World feminist, emphasises the fact that the natural wealth of these Indian and other Third World people eventually ends up here in her own backyard; that is, in the countries of the North. The imposition of a Western economic paradigm in the name of 'development' and 'progress', which emphasises industrialisation and market mechanisms, has laid out the basic economic structure whereby 'stolen' resources from other countries end up creating wealth in the North.

In her article, 'Consumption Patterns of the North – the Cause of Environmental Destruction and Poverty in the South', Mies explores and critiques the North's assumed privilege from several perspectives. It has led her to conclude that the root of deprivation is deeply embedded 'in here', in the First World, not 'out there', in the Third World, as depicted earlier by 'male' mainstream development theorists.

Mies, as well as Shiva, understands development as the continuation of colonialism. But this understanding comes from the perspective of a woman who lives in an affluent society, which makes her argument even more poignant: the process of colonisation under the mask of development has to be maintained for the sake of consumerism and present living standards in the North.

---

[2] At this point, Mies suggested that her book, *Patriarchy and Accumulation on a World Scale*, preceded that of Shiva. Her book appeared first in 1986; *Staying Alive* was published in 1989. Therefore, Mies did not respond to Shiva – 'it was rather the other way round' (letter dated 21 January 1995). However, I prefer to keep it as it is ('In response to … Shiva…'); as in this specific part of the chapter, I made many references based on Mies's article 'Consumption Patterns of the North', which came out in 1991.)

Referring to Trainer's research from his popular book, *Developed to Death: Rethinking Third World Development*, Mies uses energy consumption as an example to argue that:

> if we keep in mind that the 6 per cent of the world's population who live in the USA annually use up 30 per cent of the fossil energy produced, then it should be clear, that the rest of the world's population, of which about 75–80 per cent live in the poor countries of the South, cannot consume as much energy per person … the people living in the rich industrialised countries – USA, Europe and Japan – who make up only one quarter of the world's population, consume three quarters of the world's energy production (1991:1–2).

Therefore, Mies, quoting Trainer, summarizes that 'if present energy production were to be shared equally, Americans would have to get by on only one fifth of the per capita amount they presently consume' (ibid).

The author directly challenges Rostow's stages-of-growth model which proposes that traditional societies are in the precondition stage prior to gearing up to the advanced stage of the goods and services economy as in the Western countries. In her opinion, development is not just a simple 'catching up' or evolutionary process moving from the bottom rung of the ladder to the top, but is instead a 'polarising process' which creates 'two extreme poles of an inherently exploitative world order, divided up and yet linked by the global accumulation process of the world market' (1989: 39). As she explains,

> … since the rise of Europe and later the USA as the dominant centres of the capitalist world economy, a process of polarisation and division has been taking place by which one pole – the Western industrialised world – is getting richer and ever more powerful, and the other pole – the colonised countries in Africa, Asia and Latin America – are getting poorer and less powerful (ibid).

Development is based on exploitative and oppressive relations similar to the dynamic in men–women relations 'in
which a process of polarisation takes place: one pole is getting
"developed" *at the expense* of the other pole, which in this
process is getting "underdeveloped"' (ibid). As the author
argues,

> 200 years ago the Western world was only five times as rich
> as the poor countries of today. In 1960 this relationship was
> already 20:1 and in 1983 it was 46:1....
>
> ... it would take about 500 years till the poor countries
> would have reached the standard of living prevailing in the
> rich countries of the North. And this would only be possible
> if these rich countries would not continue with their further
> growth of goods and services (1991: 3, 2).

Another thing that needs to be taken into consideration is
that Rostow's growth model assumes that the world must
have an unlimited supply of resources. Therefore, the
advanced stage or 'catch-up' phase can never be attained by
the countries of the South as the world's resources are not only
unevenly distributed, but also limited. What is more, Mies
further challenges that '[t]he wealth in the rich countries
grows even faster and within a limited world this means it
grows at the expense of others, of what I continue to call
colonies: nature, women, the so-called Third World' (ibid).

The colonies of the South help supply and maintain the high
living standard in the rich Northern countries not only with
natural resources but also cheap labour. As Mies points out,
'... if all labour, incorporated in the commodities sold in the
rich countries was paid at the rates of a skilled (male) worker
of Germany then most of these commodities would be so
expensive that only a small minority could buy them' (ibid).

Increasing surplus from the colonies, which is then accumulated in the North, is reflected in changes in the individual's
consumption pattern and lifestyle in these rich countries. Mies

uses her home country as an example to illustrate this recent phenomenon:

> [i]n West Germany ... the consumption of private house-holds has shown a continuous growth in the last decades. Between 1950 and 1980 private consumption grew five-fold. This continuous growth of private consumption was accompanied by a change in the consumption patterns. Whereas around 1950 almost half of the expenses were spent on food this proportion was only 23 per cent in 1987. A much greater part of the income of private households could now be spent on leisure time activities and luxury items. There are, of course, also differences in the consumption patterns between lower and higher income groups, but compared to the poor countries in the world even these were relatively better off. Even the low income household spent 10.2 per cent of their expenditure on leisure time goods and activities (ibid: 34).

The growth model has brought to the North not only an accumulation of 'wealth' but also increased 'waste' in both the domestic and public spheres which have directly affected the global environmental systems through ozone-layer depletion, increases in atmospheric CO_2 (the green-house effect), and the polluting of the earth's water, soil and air with both organic and toxic wastes. In addition, Mies has compiled supporting statistical evidence regarding the deterioration of the natural environment. For example, in West Germany within a ten-year period (1971–82) household waste had more than doubled from 350 to 775 kg per person per year (ibid). In addition, to reiterate, although the industrialised countries make up only one quarter of the world's population, they collectively consume up to 75 per cent of the world's energy and produce 80 per cent of the total CO_2 emissions (ibid). The result of this tremendous increase in industrial and domestic waste in the affluent countries is that they can no longer find adequate dump-sites. As a result, the poorer countries are pushed deeper into crisis with double exploitation; they are exploited not only for their human and natural resources but they are also exploited by becoming the 'garbage colonies' for the North. For example, Canada is accused of being one of the 'sinister seven' countries, exporting over 162,000 tonnes of hazardous waste under the pretext of 'recycling', to eight Southeast Asian countries.[3] Therefore, according to Mies, to continue with efforts advanced by the current mainstream development model, which she argues is based on a more complex and exhaustive exploitative relationship with the colonies, would hypothetically require that:

> one would need two more planets if one would try to generalize the living standard and consumption patterns of the rich countries to all people living in the world: one planet to get the necessary raw materials and the other planet to dump our waste (ibid: 5).

After having persuasively presented her argument, Mies concludes:

> ... 'catching up development' is not possible for the poor countries and a conception like sustainable development for all is not comparable with a growth-oriented industrial world market system. This system is simply not sustainable.

---

[3] The above information was compiled by Greenpeace, London. *Now*, a Toronto weekly newspaper, further reports from figures provided by Canada Customs to Statistics Canada, that '... from January to October 1993, Canada exported 483,679 kilograms of ash containing lead to Taiwan, and the US [exported] 378,553 kilograms of ash containing zinc to India and other countries....' This is in contradiction with Environment Canada who reported that 'we have not exported to developing countries for final disposal or recovery since November 26, 1992' (10–16 February 1994: 13).

And it is not generalizable ... the continuation of the industrial growth model will not only lead to further ecological
destruction but also to more inequality, to more poverty.
And this will effect [sic], as is well known, women and
children first (ibid).

Through her analysis, Mies discloses the facts covered over
by the rhetoric of mainstream theories regarding their pre-
sumption that they are 'helping' the poor. She subverts the
privileged knowledge assumed by 'male' stream theorists by
reversing their emphasis on the 'quantity (of goods and
services) in life', using studies on Northern consumption
patterns from which to critique the concept of development,
and instead emphasises the more life-affirming 'quality of
life':

> ... one may ask, whether this model of the good life, pur-
> sued by the societies in the North, this paradigm of
> 'catching-up-development' has at least made people in the
> North happy. Has it in fact fulfilled its promises there? Has
> it at least made women and children there more equal, more
> free, more happy? Has their quality of life improved while
> the GDP grows? (ibid: 6).

No, it has not. Rather, there 'seems to be an inverse relationship between the GDP and the quality of life: the more the
GDP grows, the more the quality of life deteriorates'[4] (Trainer,

---

[4] On this point Shiva, quoting Port, explains in terms of the relation between
GNP and ecology that:

> GNP measures the lot, all the goods and services produced in the
> money economy. Many of these goods and services are not beneficial to
> people, but rather a measure of just how much is going wrong;
> increased spending on crime, on pollution, on the many human casual-
> ties of our society, increased spending because of waste or planned
> obsolescence, increased spending because of growing bureaucracies:
> it's all counted.

The author herself continues with the argument that:

quoted in Mies, 1991: 7). What also appears to parallel industrial growth is an increasing 'isolation and loneliness of individuals, the indifference and atomization of the society. Market forces destroy ... the communities' (ibid).

Western societies have come to the stage where 'we live on islands of affluence in a sea of poverty' (Trainer, 1989: 37). The situation on those islands, as depicted by Mies, is such that 'human dignity was destroyed in the midst of plenty of material commodities.... "Water, water all around and not a drop to drink"' (1989: 21). The destruction of the community has occurred in many different ways. Socially, one can observe this from the increases in shelterlessness, poverty, criminality, drug addiction, shopping addiction, suicide, depression, social abuse, violence against women and children, etc.

Physically, behind the rhetoric that continues to advance the desire for material wealth lies the more sober reality that affluent society desperately lacks life's fundamental necessities such as unpoisoned air, unpolluted water, healthy food, space and time, etc. What is worse is that the current economic models that unabashedly promote a lifestyle of conspicuous consumption implicitly requires the use of force as a necessary strategy for taking control of scarcer resources. The Gulf War is a clear-cut example of how force is used to secure energy reserves necessary to maintain current consumption patterns in Northern countries at the expense of many Middle Eastern

[4] (cont.) [t]he problem with GNP is that it measures some costs as benefits (e.g. pollution control) and fails to measure other costs completely. Among these hidden costs are the new burdens created by ecological devastation, costs that are invariably heavier for women, both in the North and South. It is hardly surprising, therefore, that as GNP rises, it does not necessarily mean that either wealth or welfare increase proportionately. I would argue that GNP is becoming, increasingly, a measure of how real wealth – the wealth of the nature and that produced by women for sustaining life – is rapidly decreasing (1990: 6–7).

countries who instead suffered irredeemable man-made disasters.

In addition, Mies has not only argued why and how this kind of development model is unethical, unecological and undesirable, but she has also developed strategies for making changes through a bottom-up 'consumer liberation movement', whose aim would be to improve the quality of life. This suggests that any kind of real and lasting change would primarily involve the consumers themselves, requiring a deliberate and drastic change in their lifestyle, a voluntary reduction of living standards, a change in the quantities consumed and consumer patterns, and a deliberate and broad movement geared toward energy conservation but in a way that would not engender hypocrisy:

> [i]f sustainability is a good thing for people living in the poor countries then it must also be a good thing for people living in the rich countries. A double standard is not acceptable. We cannot preach to the people in Brazil not to destroy their rainforest while we in the rich countries continue to destroy the world's climate by an ever growing car industry and private transport system (ibid: 9).

To bring about this kind of change is definitely not an easy task. Mies optimistically proposes that a consumer liberation movement could happen if a number of different steps and approaches were to be followed. They are, for example: reappropriating basic human needs and values, recreating a 'moral economy' and rethinking critical consumer action and education. However, it is beyond the scope of this book to discuss the issues of strategies and tactics of a consumer liberation movement. I will only touch upon the issue of re-appropriating basic human needs and values as it relates to the mainstream development strategy mentioned earlier.

Regarding reappropriating basic human needs and values, the author strongly believes that such changes in consumptive lifestyle will never take place within the privileged countries and classes until people start seeing a concrete connection between consumerism and the deterioration of the quality of life. This would encourage them to see that *'less is more'* (emphasised by Mies, ibid: 10–11), initiating them into identifying with a set of values and beliefs different from what had been previously promoted by self-interested business corporations.

In contrast to their materially overdeveloped condition, the affluent society is 'underdeveloped' and deficient in terms of values that need to be rediscovered and restored. These values include:

> … self-sufficiency, cooperation with other people and nature instead of competitiveness, respect for all creatures on the earth and their diversity, belief in the subjectivity not only of human beings but also of non-human beings, communality instead of aggressive self-interest of individuals, creativity instead of 'catching up with the Jones'…. Satisfaction and joy in one's work, happiness instead of standard of living, joy of life that springs from cooperation with others and an understanding in the meaningfulness of what one does (ibid).

Moreover, the concept of a 'basic needs' approach is a vital issue that should be explored further by such a consumer liberation movement. As the author proposes, 'I find the distinction between needs and satisfiers useful for our discussion on consumer liberation, because it allows us to see that there are different ways to satisfy the same fundamental human needs' (ibid). Mies, quoting from Max-Neef's (*et al.*) study, places basic human needs into nine categories:

> Subsistence (health, food, shelter, clothing etc.), Protection (care, solidarity, work etc.), Affection (self-esteem, love, care, solidarity etc.), Understanding (study, learning, analysis etc.), Participation (responsibilities, sharing of rights and

duties), Idleness (curiosity, imagination, games, relaxation, fun), Creation (intuition, imagination, work, curiosity etc.), Identity (sense of belonging, differentiation, self-esteem, etc.), Freedom (autonomy, self-esteem, self-determination, equality)... (ibid.).

They also reinforce that 'fundamental human needs are universal, but that their *satisfiers*, the means and ways [of] how these needs are satisfied, may vary according to culture, region, historical conditions' (emphasised by Mies, ibid). In a capitalist industrial society, where the organising principle of goods production is the maximisation of profits through market forces, commodities have become dominant satisfiers for fulfilling any kind of satisfaction physically or mentally. For example, Mies elaborates that in order to satisfy their need to be loved, many women buy cosmetics and the latest fashion to attract their partners. However, the simple fact is that the need for affection and self-esteem can never be fulfilled by putting on more cosmetics. These commodities are often pseudo-satisfiers which cannot satisfy more 'basic' or 'life-affirming' needs and they also bring a destructive dimension to one's life. Therefore, one of the most challenging tasks in a consumer liberation movement is to search for or create non-commercial or subsistent ways to satisfy their needs. For example, the reciprocal process of spending more time with children instead of buying more toys will satisfy both sides in many different ways, i.e. the need for affection, for protection, for understanding, etc. (ibid: 13).[5]

---

[5] Mies's proposal regarding the consumer liberation movement seems very ambiguous. There are still many questions to be discussed; for example, what about working women who cannot afford to buy toys but also cannot spend much time with their children because they have to work? What are the conditions of the working poor in the North? How can they participate in a consumerist movement? Unfortunately, it's beyond the scope of this book to explore this issue.

The way Maria Mies recontextualises the idea of basic needs into the context of consumerism is strikingly creative. It offers a new dimension in critiquing development, therefore it is worth discussing.

Historically, the implementation of basic needs strategies to alleviate world poverty has been an underlying theme of development theory since the 1950s. However, approaches targeted specifically to meet basic needs did not emerge until the 1970s. Since then the basic needs approach to development has been adopted in various degrees by a number of international agencies, such as the World Bank, ILO, FAO, UNICEF and UNESCO as well as several Third World governments (who have incorporated such strategies into their National Development Plans) (Sutherland, 1993 :3).

It is commonly understood that the development strategies of basic needs is primarily geared toward acquiring a 'minimal level of physical well-being such as adequate health, nutrition, shelter, safety and education' (ibid: 1). However, what basic needs is and how it should be achieved remains controversial: there are about as many opinions on this subject as there are agencies and Western development scholars concerned with this issue. For example, Streeten considers the acquisition of basic needs of all people, everywhere, 'to be a humanitarian aim and central to the definition of development' (ibid: 4). He calls for the provision of 'opportunities for the full physical, mental and social development of the human personality and then to derive ways of achieving this objective' (Streeten *et al.*, 1981: 33). Len Doyal and Ian Gough consider a different view of basic needs, understanding it as the 'right' to carry out social 'duties' and 'address global redistribution and concern for environmental sustainability as part of the criteria for determining needs' (Sutherland, 1993: 89).

However, critiquing basic needs as a concept, which is deeply rooted in the paternalism of Western patriarchal ideology, did not arise until the recent emergence of a new stream of alternative development thinkers, such as Thierry Verhelst and Denis Goulet.

Instead of letting development experts from developed countries define what basic needs should be for the poor in developing countries, Verhelst offers the following challenge:

> [t]he aim in matters of international cooperation for development is that everyone should have not only the *right* to live, but also *reasons* to live. Every human group must be able to draw these reasons from its own ethos. Each society's material life must, at the risk of fatal disasters, be founded on the basis of its own indigenous culture (his emphasis; 1990: 62).

However, Goulet would add that such changes cannot be met through development efforts but by a process of socio-political liberation. This is because development remains a 'pejorative' concept which 'does not evoke asymmetrical power relations operative in the world' (1979: 381). Therefore, socio-political change can only be adequately achieved by liberating oneself from these power relations. As he continues, 'for liberationists, ... success is not measured simply by the quantity of benefits gained, but above all by the way in which change processes take place' (ibid: 382).

As these two theorists seem to imply, there are two broad theoretical directions in the 'male' stream basic needs literature. To the predominant group belong those Western scholars who try to (morally) define what basic needs should be for the people in non-Western countries. The other minority group is concerned with critiquing the former groups' theories and strategies from alternate political and cultural perspectives. However, Mies goes beyond these strategies of defining and critiquing, and instead breaks through to a new level by recontextualising the basic needs approach, arguing that the current pattern of consumption in capitalist society is the root cause of deprivation in the so-called developing countries. She also provides a provocative and alternative analysis that attempts to explain how capitalism's process of accumulation operated during the colonial, and later the development era through the interplay of sexual division of labour, in terms of housewifisation, and the international division of labour.

It is of interest to learn that both leading feminists, Vandana Shiva and Maria Mies, base their critique of development on the analysis of the relation between capitalism and colonialism. However, while Shiva explores this relation from an ecological perspective in terms of natural resource utilisation for commodity production and capital accumulation, Mies believes that 'the concept which more than any others has shaped life in capitalist patriarchy is the *concept of labour*' (her italic; 1989: 212). Additionally, as capitalism constitutes the most recent and most universal manifestation of patriarchal civilisation, she also intentionally uses the terminology 'capitalist patriarchy' to denote the system whereby men continue to dominate and maintain their oppression and exploitation over women. As she explains, 'it is my thesis that capitalism cannot function without patriarchy, that the goal of this system, namely the never ending process of capital accumulation, cannot be achieved unless patriarchal man–woman relations are maintained or newly created' (ibid: 38).

Under the direction of a feminist analysis of labour, Mies tries to trace 'the [historical] processes and policies by which other countries and women are defined as "nature", or made into colonies to be exploited by WHITE MAN in the name of capital accumulation or progress and civilisation' (ibid: 4). She then extends her analysis to include the current international division of labour in which she claims the process of housewifisation has been used as a key strategy to integrate women worldwide into participating in the global accumulation of capital.

In her well-received book, *Patriarchy and Accumulation on a*

World Scale, Mies suggests that the concept of development is more or less a system, rooted in the advent of colonialism, for consumerism and capital accumulation on a world-wide scale, particularly as it is dependent upon the on-going exploitation of women. This exploitation reveals itself in a variety of forms: for example, in the unpaid work of housewives, underpaid female factory labour, and the creation of goods and services aimed at the housewife (in the role of both 'mother' and 'sexual object'). However, in addition, '... we cannot understand the modern developments, including our present problems, unless we include *all* those who were "defined into nature" by the modern capitalist patriarchs: Mother Earth, Woman and Colonies' (my emphasis; ibid: 75).

The processes by which nature was exploited and put under man's domination, the persecution of the witches in Europe, the growth and enforcement of slavery and the destruction of subsistence economies in the colonies were the 'underground connections' for the construction of capitalist patriarchy. As she explains:

> ... the rise of modern science and technology was based on the violent attack and rape of Mother Earth – hitherto conceived as a living organism. Francis Bacon, the father of modern science, was one of those who advocated the same violent means to rob Mother Nature of her secrets – namely, torture and inquisition – as were used by Church and State to get at the secrets of the witches. The taboos against mining, digging holes in the womb of Mother Earth, were broken by force, because the new patriarchs wanted to get at the precious metals and other 'raw-materials' hidden in the 'womb of the earth'. The rise of modern science, a mechanistic and physical world-view, was based on the killing of nature as a living organism and its transformation into a huge reservoir of 'natural resources' or 'matter', which could be analysed and synthesised by Man into his

new machines by which he could make himself independent of Mother Nature.

The modern European patriarchs made themselves independent of their *European* Mother Earth, by conquering first the Americas, later Asia and Africa, and by extracting gold and silver from the mines of Bolivia, Mexico and Peru and other 'raw materials' and luxury items from the other lands. They 'emancipated' themselves, on the one hand, from their dependence on European women for the production of labourers by destroying the witches, as well as their knowledge of contraceptives and birth control. On the other hand, by subordinating grown African men and women into slavery, they thus acquired the necessary labour power for their plantations in America and the Caribbean (her italic; ibid: 75–6).

Historically, from the sixteenth century onward, the world has been progressively divided into regions, economically linked to each other through many different forms of labour and production relations. This structural division of labour and production relations, reflecting 'the vertical relationship existing between the colonial powers and their dependent colonies in Africa, Latin America and Asia' (ibid: 112), is described in terms of the concept of the International Division of Labour (IDL) and the recognition that this division takes place within two distinctive periods: the 'old' and the new'. The 'old' IDL represents 'the colonial period [that] lasted almost up to the seventies of this century' (ibid), whereupon it was replaced by the new IDL.

The organising principle of the old IDL was determined by requirements for obtaining 'cheap' raw materials, which were extracted with the use of 'cheap' labour from the colonies and ex-colonies, needed by and imported to the industrialised countries. 'Expensive' labour in the industrialised countries is then used to transform the raw materials into consumer products to be marketed either domestically or exported. In sum, Mies has concluded that the key characteristic of the old IDL is that

> labour did not have the same value in the colonies and in the metropoles. In the colonies, labour costs were kept low partly by force (for example, in plantations), by a system of slave labour, by other forms of labour control (for example, indentureship) which prevented the emergence of the free wage-labourer, the prototype of the industrial worker in the West (ibid).

Generally, the old IDL simply refers to the period of direct colonialism where colonies were exploited for the sake of increasing and maintaining affluence in the metropoles. As Paul von Hindenburg, who later became German 'Reichs-kanzler', argued, '[w]ithout colonies [there can be] no security regarding the acquisition of raw materials, without raw materials no industry, without industry no adequate standard of living and wealth. Therefore, Germans, do we need colonies[?]' (Mamozai quoted in Mies, 1989: 98). Therefore, while this on-going exploitative process has brought ever growing impoverishment to the margins, in the centre, this relationship has led to ever increasing affluence, 'accompanied by greater wage demands of the workers who were also participating in the growing wealth based on the exploitation of the colonies and their workers' (ibid: 113).

However, it was not just the 'visible external' exploitation of foreign lands for raw materials and labour power by 'Big White Men', which 'was justified as a *civilising mission* of the Christian nations' (her italic, ibid: 90), that constituted the Empire's glory. But it was also the 'invisible internal' colony, the 'Little White Men's housewife and nuclear family', which played a crucial role in this global process of accumulation.

What is the historical and social construction of the nuclear family and housewife? Why? How? By and for whom? What is the function of housework in the process of global capital accumulation? What discussions have been offered on this issue? By whom? In her extensive study on the relation between colonialism, women and housework, Mies concludes that

> ... housewifization means the externalisation, or exterritorialisation of costs which otherwise would have to be covered by the capitalists. This means women's labour is considered a natural resource, freely available like air and water (ibid: 110).

Historically, housewifisation or the process of domesticating and ideologically manipulating women into their 'natural' vocation of 'wifehood' and 'motherhood' in their 'family' arena, was initially created by the European bourgeoisie around the time of the slave trade period (1655–1838). Mies, quoting Rhoda Reddock, explains that it was at exactly the same time (beginning around 1760 and lasting until about 1800) that women slaves in the Caribbean were not allowed to marry or to have children as 'it was cheaper to purchase than to breed'[6] (ibid: 91). Meanwhile, back in their homelands, women of the 'civilised' colonisers rose to the status of 'good women' or 'ladies' in order to be 'pure, monogamous breeders of their heirs, exclud[ing] them from [doing] work outside their house and from [owning] property' (ibid: 90). As she argues:

---

[6] The coloniser's attitude toward female slaves was obviously rooted in cost–benefit thinking. For example, it has found that

> [i]n the French colony of St. Dominique the planters calculated that a slave woman's work over a period of 18 months was worth 600 Livres. The 18 months were the time calculated for pregnancy and breast feeding. During such a time the slave woman would be able to do only half her usual work. Thus, her master would lose 300 Livres (ibid: 91).

[i]t was the bourgeoisie which established the social and sexual division of labour, characteristic of capitalism. The bourgeoisie declared 'family' a private territory in contrast to the 'public' sphere of economic and political activity. The bourgeoisie first withdrew 'their' women from this public sphere and shut them into their cosy 'homes' from where they could not interfere in the war-mongering, money-making and the politicking of the men (ibid: 104).

Therefore, the concept of family originates with the bourgeoisie. What we understand today as the monogamous nuclear family, which '… was put under the specific protection of the state, consists of the forced combination of the principles of kinship and cohabitation, and the definition of the man as "head" of this household and "breadwinner" for the non-earning legal wife and their children' (ibid), is definitely rooted in a sexist ideology of social relations.

In addition, another timely study on recent family history by Heinsohn and Knieper reveals that

> … the concept [of] 'family' became popular only toward the end of the eighteenth century in Europe, particularly in France and England, and it was not before the middle of the nineteenth century that this concept was also adopted for the households of the workers and peasants….
>
> …
>
> In Germany … there existed a number of marriage restrictions for people without property. These were only abolished in the second half of the nineteenth century, when the state intervened to promote a pro-natalist policy for the propertyless working class (quoted in Mies, 1989: 104).

Before the second half of the nineteenth century, the accession to have a family was considered a social privilege because 'only classes with property could afford to have a "family"' (ibid). Additionally, the concept of family '... had never existed among the propertyless farm servants or proletarians...' (ibid: 106). Many of the poor women, who constituted the cheapest and the most manipulable labour force in the early industrial period, '... did not live in proper "families", but were either unmarried, or had been deserted and lived, worked and moved around with children and young people in gangs' (Marx, quoted in Mies, 1989: 105). These women, who were overburdened with backbreaking jobs under deteriorating work conditions, had no interest in producing another generation of suffering workers for the factories. Additionally, 'women whose health had been destroyed by overwork and appalling work conditions could not produce healthy children who could become strong workers and soldiers – as was realized after several wars later in the century' (ibid).

Realising that the health of the labour force was in major crisis both economically and politically, the state, from the middle of the nineteenth century, started forcing the proletariat to form families and to take control of the latter's population production through 'legislation, police measures and the ideological campaign of the churches' (ibid). Therefore, the ideology and practice of housewifisation had been extended to cover proletariat women with the purpose of 'ensuring that there were enough workers and soldiers for capital and the state' (ibid: 106). Moreover,

[t]he creation of housework and housewife as an agent of consumption became a very important strategy in the late nineteenth and early twentieth centuries. By that time not only had the household been discovered as an important market for a whole range of new gadgets and items, but also scientific home-management had become a new ideology for the further domestication of women. Not only was the housewife called on to reduce the labour power costs, she

was also mobilized to use her energies to create new needs. A virtual war for cleanliness and hygiene – a war against dirt, germs, bacteria, and so on – was started in order to create a market for the new products of the chemical industry. Scientific home-making was also advocated as a means of lowering the men's wage, because the wage would last longer if the housewife used it economically (Ehrenreich and English, quoted in Mies, 1989: 106).

However, it was not only the bourgeoisie, through the mechanism of the state, that had placed tremendous effort into the process of housewifisation that served to 'domesticate' the female proletariat; the working-class movement in the nine-teenth and twentieth centuries had also made a crucial contribution to this process by uncritically adopting the bourgeoisie's standard of marriage and family as 'progressive' values. The German working class, according to Heinsohn and Knieper, fought for the 'freedom for workers to form a family' rather than against the 'forced celibacy of propertyless people' (quoted in Mies, 1989: 106). What is more, 'the struggles of the workers' movement for higher wages were often justified, particularly by the skilled workers who constituted the "most advanced section" of the working class, by the argument that the man's wage should be sufficient to maintain a family so that his wife could stay at home and look after children and household' (ibid: 106–7). Thus, the outcome of this process was that

… the Little White Man also got his 'colony', namely, the family and a domesticated housewife. This was a sign that, at last, the propertyless proletarian has risen to the 'civi-lized' status of a citizen, that he had become a full member of a 'culture-nation'. This rise, however, was paid for by the subordination and housewifization of the women of his class. The extension of bourgeois laws to the working class meant that in the family the propertyless man was also lord and master (ibid: 110).

However, the process of housewifization, according to Mies, could never have existed without colonization. These two processes are 'closely and causally interlinked' as she explains:

Without the ongoing exploitation of external colonies – formerly as direct colonies, today within the new international division of labour – the establishment of the 'internal colony', that is, a nuclear family and a woman maintained by a male 'breadwinner', would not have been possible (ibid).

Mies's analysis delivers a critique that at bottom argues that 'the working class as a whole had no material interest in the creation of the nuclear family and the housewifization of women' (Heinsohn and Knieper, quoted in Mies, 1989: 109). In her opinion, 'working-class women had nothing to gain, but working-class men had' (ibid) for at least two reasons. First of all, this domesticating process brings a double burden to the female working class. Few wives could afford to remain at home doing only unpaid housework while waiting to be fed by their husbands' wages; instead, most have had to do both formal and informal tasks inside and outside their families. As described by Bebel:

[t]he wife of the worker who comes home in the evening, tired and exhausted, again has her hands full of work. She has to rush to attend to the most necessary tasks. The man goes to the pub and finds there the comfort he cannot find at home, he drinks, ... perhaps he takes to the vice of gambling and loses thereby, even more than by drinking. Meanwhile the wife is sitting at home, grumbling, she has to work like a brute ... this is how disharmony begins ... (quoted in Mies, 1989: 108).

Secondly, the privatisation of their female companions has brought a material interest to the male proletarian. This refers to

> ... on the one hand, in the man's claim to monopolize available wage work, on the other, in the claim to have control over all money income in the family. Since money has become the main source and embodiment of power under capitalism, proletarian men fight about money not only with the capitalists, but also with their wives. Their demand for a family wage is an expression of this struggle. Here the point is not whether a proper family wage was ever paid or not ... the point is that the ideological and theoretical consequence of this concept led to the *de facto* acceptance of the bourgeois concept of the family and of women by the proletariat (ibid: 109).

Mies further elaborates that 'Marx's analysis of the value of labour power is also based on this concept, namely, that the worker has a "non-working" housewife.... After this all female work is devalued, whether it is wage-work or housework' (ibid: 110). Additionally it creates

> ... the total atomization and disorganization of these hidden workers. This is not only the reason for the lack of women's political power, but also for their lack of bargaining power. As the housewife is linked to the wage-earning breadwinner, to the 'free' proletarian as a non-free worker, the 'freedom' of the proletarian to sell his labour power is based on the non-freedom of the housewife. Proletarianization of men is based on the housewifization of women (ibid).

Housewifisation, or the appropriation of housework in the process of capital accumulation, is a timely turning point in the critique on the study of colonialism and capitalism. It is the area of analysis which was ignored and excluded by the 'Father' of Marxism, Karl Marx, and later by others from the orthodox left whose analysis of housework often concluded that it was merely a 'non-productive' or 'non-wage' activity which took place in a 'private' not 'public' sphere (ibid: 31–2).

In fact, several feminists have persuasively argued against such a narrow Marxist view when they claim that '… the capitalist mode of production was not identical to the capital-wage-labour relation, but that it needed different categories of colonies, particularly women, other peoples and nature, to uphold the model of ever expanding growth' (ibid: 35). However, historically, the issue of the appropriation of house-work by and for the maintenance of the processes of capital accumulation was not given any consideration until the early 1970s when Maria-Rosa Dalla Costa, an Italian feminist, challenged the classical Marxist concept of housework as 'non-productive' work in her essay ' The Power of Women and the Subversion of the Community'. Mies summarises Dalla Costa's argument as follows:

> … what the housewife produces in the family are not simple use-values but the commodity 'labour power' which the husband then can sell as a 'free' wage labourer in the labour market.… the productivity of the housewife is the pre-condition for the productivity of the (male) wage labourer. The nuclear family, organized and protected by the state, is the social factory where this commodity 'labour power' is produced. Hence, the housewife and her labour are not out-side the process of surplus value production, but constitute the very foundation upon which this process can get started.
>
> The housewife and her labour are, in other words, the basis of the process of capital accumulation. With the help of the state and its legal machinery women have been shut

up in the isolated nuclear family, whereby their work there was made socially invisible, and was hence defined – by Marxist and non-Marxist theoreticians – as 'non-productive'. It appeared under the form of love, care, emotionality, motherhood and wifehood (ibid: 31).

Dalla Costa also rejects classical Marxist assumptions regarding the issue of women's liberation, which was first addressed by Engels and later adopted by all communist parties; that is, that 'women had to leave the "private" household and enter "social production" as wage-workers along with the men if they wanted to create the preconditions for their emancipation' (ibid).

In identifying 'the strategic link created by capital and state between the unpaid housework of women and the paid wage-work of men' (ibid), she has persuasively argued that 'capital is able to hide behind the figure of the husband, called "breadwinner", with whom the woman, called "housewife", has to deal directly and for whom she is supposed to work out of "love", not for a wage' (ibid: 32). Thus, 'the wage commands more work than what collective bargaining in the factories shows us. *Women's work appears as personal service outside of capital*' (quoted in Mies, ibid).

In addition Dalla Costa has not only argued that '… one cannot understand the exploitation of wage-labour unless one understands the exploitation of non-wage-labour' (ibid); she has also rejected 'the artificial division and hierarchy capital has created between wage-workers on the one side and non-wage-workers on the other' (ibid):

In the measure that capital has subordinated the man to itself by making him a wage-labourer it has created a cleavage between him – the wage labourer – and all other proletarians who do not receive a wage. Those who are not considered capable of becoming a subject of social revolt because they do not participate directly in social production (quoted in Mies, ibid).

Finally, Dalla Costa concludes that '… the family and the household … is a colony, dominated by the "metropolis", capital and state' (quoted in Mies, ibid). Therefore, in comparison, women's struggles as housewives and non-wage-workers, as an expression of the sexual division of labour resulting from the colonisation process, are structurally similar to 'the struggles of Third World countries against imperialism as well as that [sic] of the blacks in the United States and the youth rebellion as the revolt of all those who had been defined as being *outside* of capitalism…' (ibid).

In addition, she has provided new direction in this area of study by drawing attention to the lack of any critical analysis on the significance and necessity of housework in the processes of capitalism; that is, the finding that wage labour is not the 'only' capitalist production relation as there is the non-wage labour such as housework which 'was the mechanism by which it became a "colony" and a source for unregulated exploitation' (ibid: 33). Such an analysis opens up critical areas for further analysis on other such colonies of non-wage labour exploitation. In addition, Mies and two other German feminists, Werlhof and Bennholdt-Thomsen, have put together a study on the various forms of non-wage labour relations and their place in a worldwide system of capital accumulation. In particular, by focusing on study cases of small peasants and women in Third World countries whose housework and subsistence work are crucial prerequisites for the privileged male wage-labour, their work has lent support to Rosa Luxemburg's decisive analysis:

…Marx's model of accumulation was based on the assumption that capitalism was a closed system where there were only wage labourers and capitalists. Rosa Luxemburg showed that historically such a system never existed, that capitalism had always needed what she called 'non-capitalist milieux and strata' for the extension of the labour force, resources and above all the extension of markets. These non-capitalist milieux and strata were initially the peasants and artisans with their 'natural economy', later the colonies. Colonialism … is therefore not only the last stage of capitalism … but its constant necessary condition. In other words, without colonies capital accumulation or extended reproduction of capital would come to a stop… (ibid: 34).

What is more, Mies proposes that today the most challenging feminist task is '*to include all these relations* in an analysis of women's work under capitalism' (ibid). This is because

> … there can be no doubt that capital has already reached the stage of which Rosa Luxemburg spoke. All milieux and strata are already tapped by capital in its global greed for ever-expanding accumulation. It would be self-defeating to confine our struggles and analysis to the compartmentalizations capitalist patriarchy has created: if Western feminists would only try to understand women's problems in over-developed societies, and if Third World women would only restrict their analysis to problems in underdeveloped societies. Because capitalist patriarchy, by dividing and simultaneously linking these different parts of the world, has already created a worldwide context of accumulation within which the manipulation of women's labour and the sexual division of labour plays a crucial role (ibid).

To reiterate, Mies recognises two distinct periods whereby the division of labour and its relation to the accumulation of capital took on different forms: these are the 'old' and the 'new' International Division of Labour (IDL). As she again explains:

[t]he old IDL began in the colonial period and lasted almost up to the seventies of this century.

In the 1970s, however, the managers of the big national and multinational corporations in Europe, the USA and Japan, realized that the boom period which had followed the end of World War II was over, ... the need to change the system of the world economy – or the IDL – in such a way that continuous growth would return to the capitalist countries became paramount.... This new model, worked out by the Organization for Economic Cooperation and Development (OECD), the supranational organisation of Western industrial countries, meant labour-intensive and hence labour-cost-intensive-production processes should be exported to the colonies, now called developing countries, the Third World, etc. (ibid: 113).

Mies chooses the 1970s to represent the period of transition between these two significant periods in the world economic system. However, her study would be much more thorough and insightful if she had inquired further into the 'transition' period, that is, with the emergence of the ideology and practice of 'development' at the end of the colonial period.

At this point, I found that Charoensin-o-larn's research, *Understanding Postwar Reformism in Thailand*, helped bridge the gap with his analysis of the process of global accumulation in the period between the Second World War and the 1970s (the period of transition). As he discusses:

Since the Second World War, a new ideology of *developmentalism* has spread over the so-called Third World countries. The new ideology was partially inspired by the demonstration effects of the rapid postwar economic recovery of Japan, the successful economic reconstruction of Western Europe through US aid under the Marshall Plan, and the rise of the Soviet Union from a prewar

agriculturally backward country to a postwar industrialised and a new world power. In fact, the widespread
acceptance of this new ideology has been made possible by
the major contributions of one leading core state, the USA,
and its affiliated international development agencies,
notably the World Bank, officially known as the International Bank for Reconstruction and Development (IBRD).

The form this new ideology has taken is generally
referred to as [the] 'modernisation theory'. As the name
signifies, the primary objective of [the] modernisation
theory is to provide *a path which the respective Third World
States must take in the due course of their transition from
'traditional' to 'modern' societies*. The theory gained its
momentum during the 1950s and the 1960s, when it success-
fully dominated the domain of development thinking on
the Third World (1988: 1920).

Beginning in the early 1960s, an ideology of 'developmentalism' was put into practice with the export of a strategy
of accumulation called the 'Import-Substitution Industrialisation' (ISI) to the Third World in the belief that 'the
developing countries can "catch up" with the developed
nations by simply imitating the latter's style of development,
i.e. through industrialisation' (ibid: 169). Technically, the
reason that these countries should start with this step is that
they have not yet reached the conditions necessary for
industrialisation, i.e. a high level of technological knowledge,
management skills and intensive capital, etc. Therefore, 'it
would be better for these countries to start with light
manufacturing industries geared toward the stable "home"
market by producing substitutes for the imported consumer
goods' (ibid). After almost a decade of implementing this
strategy, it was found that the weakness of ISI was not only the
limitations of the home market in the poor countries but also
their difficulties in repaying capital, loans, and purchasing

high-technology machinery from the rich countries. Therefore, the time was right for the implementation of a 'more
appropriate' development theory, that is, to move from the
inward-looking industries such as ISI, 'to pursue a high level
of industrialisation by adopting an outward-looking policy of
competing in the world market' (ibid: 170), or Export-
Oriented Industrialization (EOI). As stated in one of the World
Bank's small pamphlets entitled *Industry*:

> ... new industries oriented toward the export market can
> develop a comparative advantage only after skills and
> entrepreneurship have been acquired through production
> for domestic market.... Import substitution and a certain
> degree of protection for infant industries is *a normal and often
> indispensable initial phase in the industrialisation process*.... By
> contrast, greater emphasis on manufacturing for exports
> will permit the establishment of larger industrial units with
> economies of scale, provide access to scarce foreign
> exchange resources, and give new momentum to industrial
> development (quoted in Charoensin-o-larn, ibid: 171, his
> emphasis).

In Southeast Asia, this new strategy has been actively
adopted. The Asian Development Bank stated in one of its
reports that the focus on 'the exploitation of natural and
human resources must be intensified' and

> ... instead of orienting their industrial pattern towards their
> limited domestic markets, the Southeast Asian countries
> should orient it towards the export market and should also
> try to take advantage of their abundant endowment of natu-
> ral resources.... In order to succeed in the export of labor-
> intensive manufactures, wage-cost must be kept low....
> Potentially, the most important factor to be taken into
> account in the new strategy of industrialisation is the Green
> Revolution itself (quoted in Charoensin-o-larn, ibid: 170).

Since then, as a result, the Southeast Asian countries' economies have been tightly tied to the global accumulation of capital which not only intensified the degree of external exploitation but also strengthened the dominance of centre-periphery relations. As defined by Ichiyo:

> For the export-oriented industrialisation on the one hand internalises imperialism in the heart of the host country's economy and on the other hand links it with [the] global system of production and marketing dominated by the giant multinational corporations.... The 'export-oriented industrialisation' ... never means 'industrialisation of Asia through export promotion' but means operation reflecting the decision of multinational capital to begin its own 'competitive' business in Asia (ibid: 171).

Charoensin-o-larn's political economic analysis has filled in some missing pieces regarding the process of global capital accumulation as disseminated through the strategies of ISI and EOI under the rhetoric of 'development' during the 'transitional' period (that is, the period between the Second World War and the early 1970s). However, even though the transitional period is missing in Mies's work, her research is still extraordinarily valuable as she is able to utilise the feminist concept of labour to analyse the 'visible surface' of the system by revealing the 'invisible submerged' parts which 'constitutes the base of the whole'. This has allowed her to explain how women in both the First and the Third World have been exploited, often brutally, in order to maintain the process of accumulating capital, which she reveals lies at the heart of the paradigm of the New International Division of Labour (IDL).

What is the new IDL? What are the major consequences of these recent development approaches? Mies describes at least three different significant consequences; that is, firstly, it has created a rigid division between the sphere of global production and consumption in such a way that 'developing countries increasingly become areas of production of consumer goods for the rich countries, whereas rich countries increasingly become areas of consumption only' (1989: 114). Secondly, the operation of the EOI in the Third World countries 'gears most labour time, raw materials, skills, and technical development towards the demands of the market in the rich countries, not towards the needs of people in the under-developed countries' (ibid). The 'demands' include food and fruits, daily consumer goods, entertainment gadgets, luxury items, components for military equipment, semiconductors and microprocessors. Thirdly, as both the wages for labour and the cost for raw materials in producing these commodities are very cheap, they can be sold in the rich countries at incredibly cheap prices as 'mass consumption goods'. Therefore, in conclusion, the meaning behind the new IDL is that it 'guarantees a [high] level of mass consumption in the rich countries'; a level which, she continues to argue, would be sufficient in helping 'prevent the [possible] outbreak of social unrest' (ibid).

However, the successful implementation of the new IDL strategy will never be achieved if certain parallel conditions are not first fulfilled; that is, the mobilisation of both First and Third World women to participate from their respective ends in this process. On the one hand, the new IDL requires a strategy that can readily make available the cheapest, and the most submissive and manipulable workers in the developing countries, thereby contributing to the lowering of production costs necessary for encouraging the relocation of industries, agro-business and other export-oriented enterprises. On the other hand, as '… it is not enough that these commodities are produced as cheaply as possible, they have to be sold' (ibid: 120), female middle-class consumers in the rich countries become the target of this marketing strategy. This is because if there is no consumption of commodities, the accumulation of capital will never take place.

However, with respect to Third World women, their integration into the global market economy has taken place in four major sectors. Firstly, it is the

> large-scale manufacturing industries, mostly owned by transnational enterprises in the Free Production Zones or World Market Factories. These industries include mainly electronics, textiles and garments, and toys. Apart from these central units, there are often many small-scale ancillary units, either as small workshops or as cottage industries to which certain production processes are subcontracted... (ibid: 114–15).

The second major sector is often referred to as the 'informal sector' which is based on 'small-scale manufacturing of a variety of consumer goods, ranging from handicrafts, food processing, garment manufacture, to making art objects' (ibid). Geographically, the production units are often located either in urban slums or rural areas. Additionally, this sector had traditionally been the place where use-value items were produced for community consumption. However, in recent years, through income generating strategies, this mode of production has been integrated into the external market system to produce exchange value items as commodities.

The third sector is the agricultural sector, which is comprised of

1) large-scale cash crop production for export (for example, strawberries, flowers, vegetables);

2) women working in plantations (tea, coffee);

3) women working as unpaid 'family labour' in small peasant units which produce independently or on a contract basis for agro-business firms;

4) women working as unpaid 'family labour' within co-operatives which produce for export;

5) women working as casual labour in commercial agriculture (rice, sugar) (ibid).

The final sector is the tourist and sex industries, whose economic importance has increased tremendously in recent years.

Female labourers, because of their ubiquitous involvement in the production of commodity goods for the markets in the First World countries, constitute a very significant proportion of the labour force in the global market economy. In conclusion, what becomes evident is that

> [t]he overabundance of commodities in the Western supermarkets is not the result – as is mostly assumed – of the 'productivity' of work of the workers in the industrialized countries; this 'productivity' is itself a result of exploitation and super-exploitation of the colonies, particularly of women... (ibid: 116–17).

In fact, this is further reinforced by the United Nations who claim that 'today two-thirds of all labour in the world is done by women' (quoted in Mies, ibid). Moreover, Frobel and his associates have reported that in the Free Production Zones in Southeast Asia, Africa and Latin America, more than 70 per cent of the labour force who work on the assembly lines are females between the ages of 14 and 24 (quoted in Mies, ibid). It is their own 'pimp' governments who directly sell these women to foreign capital. For example, the Haitian government advertised that '[n]ow you get more labour for your DM. For only 1 US Dollar, she works happily for eight hours for you, and many, many hundreds of her friends will do so, too' (ibid).

In addition, Mies observes that '[a]lmost at the same time as this new international division of labour was being worked out and put into practice, the world was made aware of the necessity of "integrating women into development"' (ibid: 118). However, she challenges this by raising the question '...why, all of a sudden, women, and poor Third World women ... have been rediscovered by international capital'? (ibid: 116).

The idea for 'integrating women into development' was initially proposed by the United Nations in 1975. Since then other international agencies, especially the World Bank, have adopted and included a chapter on 'women and development' in their programmes. As the Bank states in one of its documents:

> The need to recognise and support the role of women in development is an issue which the World Bank considers of great importance for itself and its member governments. The bank expects to participate to an increasing extent in the efforts of those governments to extend the benefits of development to all of their population, women as well as men, and *thus ensure that so large a proportion of the world's human resources is not underutilised* (quoted in Mies, ibid: 122).

Mies questions further as to whether we can 'consider this as a genuine change of heart on the part of the male development planners?... And what did they, what *do* they, mean by "integrating women into development"?' (ibid: 118). Finally, she has come to realise that this new strategy of accumulation is dependent upon three substrategies which are historically, politically and economically related to and reflected in each other. These substrategies include income generating activities, international housewifisation and family planning.

First of all, Mies explains that a strategy of 'integrating women into development' means, '...in most cases, getting women to work in some so-called *income-generating activities*, that is, to enter market-oriented production' (ibid), to produce something to be sold in exchange for 'cash'. As poor Third World women have very low purchasing power, it means that they produce primarily for those city people, living either in their own countries or abroad, who have greater purchasing power. Moreover, Mies, quoting Deere (1976), further elaborates that before the arrival of the new IDL strategy, women had already been

> … integrated into the old strategy of development. Their unpaid or low paid labour as farm workers, as factory workers, as housewives, had also been the base of what has been called modernization in developing countries. But this labour had remained invisible; it provided a lot of the subsistence basis on which male wage-labour could emerge. It subsidized the male wage (ibid).

However, the arrival of the new strategy of 'integrating women into development' did not serve to help women emancipate themselves from their subordinate status, neglecting either to support them by expanding their subsistence production, or to assist them in gaining control over their own means of production (e.g. land ownership). Instead, it pushed them further into conditions of absolute poverty, as '[p]oor Third World women produce not what they need, but what others *can buy*' (ibid).

Secondly, the successful strategy of housewifisation implemented in Europe and the United States in the nineteenth and twentieth centuries has also been effectively imposed on Third World countries. Mies argues that the

> … characteristic of this strategy is that it defines Third World women *not as workers, but as house-wives*. What they do is not defined as work, but as an 'activity'. By universalizing the housewife ideology and the model of the nuclear family as

signs of progress, it is also possible to define all the work women do – whether in the formal or informal sectors – as supplementary work, her income as supplementary income to that of the so-called main 'breadwinner', the husband (ibid).

The mystification of women that occurs in the process of housewifisation helps to not only pave a smooth path for the process of capital accumulation in terms of justifying low wages, atomising women and preventing them from organising, etc., but also allows for 'a tremendous reduction of labour costs' (ibid: 119). Thirdly, in order to achieve a more efficient and successful systematisation and mystification of the purposes and processes of over-consumption in the rich countries, the myth of 'over-population', the so-called primary cause of hunger and poverty in poor countries, had been invented at the end of the 1960s (ibid: 121). To solve this imposing problem, a 'family planning' strategy was inten-tionally developed by 'the pillars of corporate capitalism and imperialism, first by the Rockefeller Foundation, the US State Department and the US Agency for International Develop-ment (AID), then by the World Bank, which sold it to a large number of Third World governments and practically to all Western governments' (ibid). As the World Bank stated in 1968:

> All such [family planning] activity arises out of the concern of the Bank for the way in which the rapid growth of population has become a major obstacle to social and economic development in many of our member states. Family Planning programs are less costly than conventional development projects and the pattern of expenditure involved is normally very different. At the same time, we are conscious of the fact that successful programs of this kind will yield very high economic returns (Hawkin, quoted in Mies, ibid: 122).

In order to translate policy into practice effectively, '[t]he World Bank put pressure on governments asking for loans to take specific social and economic action to reduce fertility and to raise the status of women, socially, economically and politically' (McNamara, quoted in Mies, ibid). From the perspective of the bank, 'raising the status of women' referred to 'educating women in order to increase their productivity, and to increasing their knowledge of contraceptives and their readiness to accept birth control measures' (ibid).

Additionally, Mies makes the observation that even though there were many 'Women and Development' programmes initiated by the International Development Agencies and exported to the countries of the South, none of them were 'interested in augmenting the consumption fund of the poor, but only in increasing the marketable output' (ibid: 123). Poor consumers and breeders 'are seen as a threat to the global system' (ibid); thus to lessen their number was the hidden agenda of this strategy. Therefore, Mies concludes that '[t]he rhetoric on integrating Third World women into development means precisely this: obfuscating women's work as producers for capital by defining them as housewives and not as workers … and by emphasizing their behaviour as "breeders" of unwanted consumers' (ibid).

The modernisation strategy of the new IDL has affected Third World women enormously. Ashok Mitra, an Indian demographer, has noted that they have been turned into

[an] expendable commodity as consumers and procreators. In the last thirty years after Independence Indian women have increasingly become an expendable commodity, expendable both in the demographic and in the economic sense. Demographically woman is more and more reduced to her reproductive functions, and when these are fulfilled she is expendable. Economically she is relentlessly pushed out of the productive sphere and reduced to a unit of

consumption which therefore is undesired (quoted in Mies, ibid).

In conclusion, what seems to be happening nowadays under the guise of 'family planning' is not much different from the witch hunts of premodern patriarchies as 'one cannot help but recognize a virtual trend towards gynocide' (ibid: 123).

Additionally, Mies proposes that there is another dimension which has been left out from the 'male' mainstream discourse on women and development; that is, the role housewives play in the overdeveloped countries and consumer classes. In her opinion, the new strategy of 'integrating women into develop-ment' does not refer to only one side of the global division of labour, that is, to mobilise 'poor, cheap, docile, dexterous, submissive Third World women for export-oriented produc-tion' (ibid: 120). The other side is to also integrate First World women into the process of consumption. This happens according to one of four ways.

First of all, as a consequence of the new IDL, women in Europe and the United States have been increasingly removed from their role as 'producers' in the 'formal sector', especially in the textile and electronics industries. They are being sent back to their kitchens to look after their households and children. At the same time, the same multinational corpora-tions (MNCs), utilising advertisements and media, especially TV and cable TV, have strategically provided them with another crucial job; that is, to be committed and loyal buyers of the products of these companies (ibid: 114, 120).

Secondly, the new IDL does not only geographically divide the world into the spheres of production and consumption but also separates women internationally and class-wise into producers and consumers. As she discusses:

This relationship is structured in such a way that Third World women are *objectively* – not *subjectively* – linked to First World women *through the commodities* which the latter buy. This is not only a contradictory relationship, but also one in which the two actors on each side of the globe do not know anything of each other. The women in the South and Southeast Asia hardly know what they produce or for whom they make the things they make. On the other hand, the Western housewife is totally oblivious of the female labour, the working conditions, the wages, etc. under which the things which she buys are produced. She is only interested in getting these things as cheaply as possible ... if we look more closely at the consequences of this strategy, we may come to another conclusion, namely, that the enslavement and exploitation of one set of women is the foundation of a qualitatively different type of enslavement of another set of women. One is the condition as well as the consequence of the other (ibid: 120–1).

Thirdly, there is not only an economic but also an ideological separation between these two groups of women, which dates as far back as the colonial period:

... while African women were treated as 'savages', the women of the white colonizers in their fatherlands 'rose' to the status of 'ladies'. These two processes did not happen side by side, are not simply historical parallels, but are intrinsically and causally linked within this patriarchal-capitalist mode of production. This creation of 'savage' and 'civilized' women, and the polarization between the two was, and still is, the organizing structural principal also in other parts of the world subjected by capitalist colonialism (ibid: 95).

The division between 'Good' and 'Bad' women nowadays is also reflected in the way 'Third World women as consumers and procreators are considered highly undesirable, even expendable' (ibid: 121), which can be clearly seen in the gynocidal character of present 'family planning' policy and practice. On the other hand, 'First World women must by all means be made to breed more (white) children than they are doing at present, and they must be made by all means to buy more goods and commodities for their family, their children, the household, and for themselves as sex objects' (ibid: 125).

Fourthly, a more recent phenomenon in the overdeveloped countries is the tremendous increase in 'consumption work'. Both wage and non-wage working women are finding that they are spending a greater amount of their free time to accomplish this work. To survive, for First World people whose lives are almost completely chained to the market system for fulfilling their basic needs, means learning to do consumption work strategically. Additionally, the situation will become aggravated with technological replacements such as robotics and computers. As Mies points out:

> Whereas some years ago the housewife had to run through the supermarkets to select the commodities, compare prices, pay the bills at the cash counter, carry the commodities home, unpack everything, store everything, remove the packing, etc., she is now already forced also to put the commodities into a bag herself, weigh them, put the price into the computer, and put the tag on her merchandise, before she can pay at the counter (ibid: 126).

By exploring both sides, Mies found that 'the way in which Third World women are at present integrated into capitalist development is the model also for the reorganisation of labour in the centres of capitalism' (ibid: 127). As she explains:

> … international capital not only rediscovered women – mainly in the underdeveloped countries – to lower the production costs, it also rediscovered women in the centres of capitalism to lower the cost of producing an adequate demand for its commodities. Increasingly, the socialized services (in health, education, information, transport)

which in many countries were paid for by the welfare state, are again being privatized. This privatization means that women's work as housewives will increase tremendously in the future (ibid: 126).

In conclusion, utilising a feminist perspective to explore the concept of 'development' through the interplay between sexual and international division of labour, Mies realises that

[t]he whole strategy is based on a patriarchal, sexist and racist ideology of women which defines women basically as housewives and sex objects. Without this ideological manipulation combined with the structural division of women by class and colonialism, this strategy would not be profitable for capital…. Not only do the BIG WHITE MEN or Mr. CAPITAL profit from the exploitation of their own women and of Third World women, so also do the small white men, the workers. Not only the Big Brown or Black Men profit from the exploitation of 'their' women, but also the small black or brown men. And the big and small white women also share in the profit from the exploitation of both small brown and black men and women in the colonies. So do the big brown or black women in the colonies who aspire to the status of the real Western housewife as a symbol of progress and who have been discovered as promoters of Third World capitalism. (ibid: 142–3).

Approaching development from a feminist critique has brought me to the realisation that there are many ways to critique development historically and philosophically. From the 'margins', Vandana Shiva has undertaken a process of recovering and bringing to the forefront the suppressed voices of rural Indian women (thereby 'rupturing' the mono-cultural discourse of Western development). From the 'centre', Maria Mies not only challenges the whole of mainstream development thinking by arguing that the root causes of deprivation are not out there but here, in the affluent society, but she also offers a critique of Western consumption and proposes ideas and approaches for making changes. However, the feminist critique of development will remain inadequate as long as it does not include one other critical aspect; that is, *to make the connection between the margin and the centre*, or the Third World and the First World, through the process of identifying and demystifying 'all colonizing divisions created by capitalist patriarchy, particularly by the interplay between the sexual and the international division of labour' (ibid: 35).

In summary, what Mies offers as an alternative to mainstream development discourse is a provocative and extraordinary approach which reveals for us the understanding that the critique of development must necessarily proceed, not only from the context of the periphery, but also from the centre. In doing so, it will not only delegitimise the presumed dominance of Western ideology, but also (re)create more open space for non-Westerners to de-colonise themselves from the imposed hegemonic Western concept of development and regain their confidence in building up their own localised 'theories' and 'strategies' for making changes.

In terms of content, the issues of 'housewifisation and international division of labour' is a crystallising critique of traditional development theories. Its critical insights have been confirmed by many other recent research studies. For example, the United Nations Publication (1991), *The World's Women 1970–1990 Trends and Statistics*, makes two important generalisations:

> [f]irst, everywhere in the world women have near total responsibility for household work. Second, men in developing regions do less, and often much less household work than men in the developed regions (quoted in Lycklama à Nijeholt, 1992: 4).

However, her thorough historical study on the changing

roles of Western women in their effort to win back their independence from the imposed subordination by men in the model of 'breadwinner-housewife', might be well suited to the context of industrialised countries. The question is how appropriate is it in helping explain the changing gender relations in other cultures. For example, in rural Thai society, there is a traditional saying that 'daughters are money-makers, sons are money-users'. Aeusrivongse, a leading Thai historian, notes that:

> Actually, in traditional Thai culture, women had a much more prominent economic role than men had. It could be said that women were the 'economic pillars' of the family whether as married women who had their own family or as single women who still lived with their parents.

> Up until even the present, rural Thais, who are less influenced by Chinese or Western culture than the urban people, still expect from their daughters, rather than their sons, the greatest share in maintaining family financial security. It is the daughter and not the son who will take care of the parents in their old age. Whenever the son gets married, he moves out, becomes his father-in-law's family member and works on their farm.

> Additionally, the son doesn't have any role in inheriting the family's spirit. The sacred duty of paying homage to their ancestors is something that will be passed on by and from mother to daughter who volunteers to carry it on (1994: 113–14, my translation).

Aeusrivongse's study makes me realise that although feminism can offer a ground-breaking critique of development discourse, it cannot be generalised to other contexts and situations. As proposed by Gita Sen and Caren Grown in *Development, Crises and Alternative Visions: Third World Women's Perspectives*:

While gender subordination has universal elements, feminism cannot be based on a rigid concept of universality that negates the wide variation in women's experience. There is and must be a diversity of feminisms, responsive to the different needs and concerns of different women, and *defined by them for themselves* (1989: 189).

Let's explore, in the following chapter, what 'development' really means to Thai women.

Women benefit from [growth] even more than men.... Woman gains freedom from drudgery, is emancipated from the seclusion of the household, and gains at last the chance to be a full human being, exercising her mind and her talents in the same way as man. It is open to men to debate whether economic progress is good for men or not, but for women to debate the desirability of economic growth is to debate whether women should have the chance to cease to be beasts of burden, and to join the human race.

ARTHUR LEWIS

4

What Does 'Development' Mean to *Us*?

What does 'development' mean to Thai women? If you ask this question of a female Thai worker who works at the Bic pen factory in the Industrial Estate near Bangkok, the answer that you get might be 'I don't care!'. Instead, what she may claim is of concern to her is that '[t]he management think we are machines. Time is important for them. We clock in and clock off and in between there is not even time to go to the toilet' (quoted in Nelson, 1989: 97).

If you ask Doaw, a bar-girl who works in Patpong, the most famous red-light district in Bangkok, the same question, she might answer 'I don't know!' However, what she does know is that

> working in Patpong is not that easy. She began as a go-go dancer, wearing a bikini and sitting with customers to get drinks. Then Doaw was forced to do bar-shows because business was slow in the bar. Doaw had to insert a variety of objects into her vagina and dance erotically while she removed them on the stage … razor blades, bananas, ping-pong balls, eggs, coloured water, cake, whistles, darts… (Apisuk *et al.*, 1987: 6).

The concept and practice of development have had different meanings for and effects on the lives of different groups of Thai women over the past three decades. In this chapter, I'd like to explore what it means to 'us', a special group of Thai women, who, in order to survive in the face of global militarism and consumerism brought on by development, have had to use their own bodies as a means of earning income. Their stories will be divided into two parts: first, an overall picture of the prostitution problem in Thailand; and then, a closer analysis.

The first step toward an overview of the issues of prostitution in Thailand requires a description of facts and figures. According to one document, prepared by the Centre for the Protection of Children's Rights for the National Commission on Women's Affairs (NCWA), in 1990 it was estimated that the overall number of prostitutes in Thailand was a staggering 2,820,000; that is, approximately 2,000,000 adult females, 800,000 girls under the age of 16 and 20,000 young males. To give some idea of its absolute magnitude, six years earlier in 1984, when the total number of prostitutes was estimated at 700,000, it was determined that up to 29 per cent of all women between the ages of 15 and 45 worked in the sex trade (ibid: 37–8). It would be expected that this percentage is much higher today. Bangkok alone, having approximately a half million prostitutes, has developed the reputation of being 'the largest brothel in Asia' (Skrobanek, 1990a: 12). This reputation may have already been surpassed judging by claims such as those made by Richard Rhodes (1991) in 'Death in the Candy Store'. Rhodes asserts that Thailand is the prostitution capital or the 'whore house' of the entire world.

The estimation of the number of prostitutes appears to be so unusually large, as well as significantly variable, that it is questionable whether we can rely on any of these estimates. The first problem, then, in doing research on prostitution is accounting for the large numerical variation in the data. For instance, while one NGO calculated that there were up to 2,820,000 prostitutes, another survey undertaken by the Ministry of Public Health between 1 and 12 January 1990, estimated that the total number of prostitutes was much less at no more than 86,494, which was expected to increase to 119,537 by the year 1996 (NCWA, 1990).

Since the estimated number of prostitutes in Thailand remains under constant debate, with a 'reliable' estimate not having been agreed upon yet, some researchers, such as Kritaya Archavanitkul, have commented that an 'approxima- tion of the number of prostitutes, both child and adult, should be undertaken with extreme caution. The population of women in each respective age group should be taken into account' (1990: 20). She herself preferred the middle estimate.

On the issue of income from prostitution, Chantawipa Apisuk estimated that 700,000 prostitutes would make 14 billion baht, or US$370 million a month. This would include the money deducted to pay off pimps, bar owners and agents, who collectively would receive no less than 30 per cent of the total. Another 5–10 per cent would go to the police.

These amounts are based on the 1984 statistics in general, but individual situations vary significantly. For instance, a beautiful masseuse could make up to 25,000 baht (US$660) a month while a 'bonded'[1] girl with a dishonest owner would be lucky to get only 500 baht (US$13) (Phongpaichit, 1982: 19). Normally, most prostitutes have to service 3–5 customers per night or 60–150 customers per month. However, this number will double or triple during the holiday seasons, such as Christmas, New Year, Chinese New Year and the traditional Thai New Year.

---

[1] 'Bonded' refers to girls who come to work at the brothels (or massage parlours) to pay back the debts of their parents, as they have already been advanced payment from the agents, procurers, or brothel owners.

Prostitution in Thailand is illegal. How can it be then that so many women continue to work as prostitutes? The answer is that it can be disguised in many different ways. There are many places where and pretexts under which prostitution operates. These include places such as hotels, teahouses, beerbars, discotheques, coffee shops, cocktail lounges, pubs, massage parlours, beauty salons, barber shops, truck stops, cattle markets. The women perform their jobs under the guise of bar hostesses, go-go dancers, waitresses, masseuses, hairdresser assistants, call-girls, escorts, etc.

Prostitutes also work in public places such as streets, parks and shopping malls, while high class prostitutes operate out of exclusive member's clubs. During the day, these women have regular office jobs, but at night they work as prostitutes. Male prostitutes work in bars, cocktail lounges, restaurants, pubs, saunas, discotheques and guesthouses. A government study found that the number of sex service businesses that were operating included 6,160 businesses for female prostitutes and another 58 for male prostitutes (NCWA, 1991). This number varies greatly from that estimated by the Centre for the Protection of Children's Rights, which was around 60,000 (quoted in Schmetzer, 1990). (If accurate, this would be more than the total number of secondary schools found throughout the entire country.)

Besides providing sex services for customers, each form of prostitution has its own set of particular activities. I will illustrate this with two examples. First, I will begin with Doaw's story. She is an eighteen-year-old sex-show worker at a bar on Patpong Street, the most famous red-light district in Bangkok. 'Patpong', which covers an area of one half kilometre square, contains over 200 bars, numerous restaurants, massage parlours and barber shops. At least 4,000 women work there on any one night (Apisuk *et al.*, 1987: 31).

Doaw comes from a family of 6 kids. Doaw's only sister is married and all of her brothers are studying at school. When Doaw was 17, she and 4 girlfriends ran away to Bangkok to search for work. They found their first jobs in a restaurant working as waitresses, earning only 500 baht a month including food but not accommodation. Then they heard about Patpong and how they could get 2,500 baht a month plus 900–1,000 baht extra in commission for drinks.

Doaw says it is an advantage to do the shows as she earns a flat 3,000 baht a month and there are no deductions (a go-go dancer's salary is usually 2,500 baht a month but they are required to be 'bought out' of the bar at least 4 times a month. If they aren't, their salary is cut by 300 baht a time).

Doaw is taking 'uppers'. She says the pills help her when she does a show and stops the pain if she cuts herself with the blades (ibid: 6).

Another classical form of prostitution, which has now become historical, is the 'rented wife' or 'hired wife', which was popular during the Vietnam war. These women cooked for the GIs, looked after their houses and took care of their personal business. During that time, the GIs, with their US dollars, could rent women as they rented houses, cars and other commodities.

However, the increasing problem of prostitution in Thailand also needs to be understood as the result of a more global phenomenon. For example, Mies, in her analysis of the strategy of integrating Third World women into development, stated that

[t]he most blatant manifestation of the combination of the new IDL with the neo-patriarchal or sexist division of labour is sex-tourism. Tourism to Third World countries, particularly in Asia, became a growth industry in the 1970s and continued to be propagated as a development strategy by international aid agencies. In fact, this industry was first

planned and supported by the World Bank, the IMF and USAID. Between 1960 and 1979, tourist arrivals in South-East Asia increased 25-fold… (1989: 137).

While the Third World governments act as 'national pimps', working cooperatively with 'global pimps', such as the World Bank, the IMF and USAID, to offer their women to foreign men, Hantrakul found that the local folks also have a very decisive function in this sexploitation process. As she stated:

> traditional brothels play a more vital role in the continuation of prostitution in the country, not only because they are more ancient but also because they have maintained the popularity of prostitution and continued to provide access to the mass of Thai males of middle class and lower classes (1988: 121).

It is undeniable, however, that foreign influence in the forms of militarism and tourism has played a very prominent role during the past few decades in making prostitution a prominent industry in Thailand.

During the Vietnam War, there were six US military airbases located in Thailand, each occupied by large numbers of GIs. Because it was directly accessible from Vietnam, many GIs would travel to Thailand to spend their seven days of R & R (Rest and Recreation). It was often instead referred to as I & I – Intercourse and Intoxication (Rhodes, 1991: 69). Most GIs chose Bangkok, instead of other destinations such as Tokyo and Sydney, because they wasted less I & I time getting there. In 1966 alone, up to 33,000 GIs came to Thailand; the figure increased to 70,000 a year for 1968–9 (Hantrakul, 1988: 129–30). It was estimated that these short-term visitors spent about 400 million baht (US $16 million) (Phongpaichit, 1982: 5). The newcomers, according to Hantrakul, 'did not corrupt a simple people but rather, by introducing an additional demand they extended facilities' (1988: 130). However, many of them did introduce new forms of sex entertainment.[2] For example, there is the story of Rick Menard, a former USAF helicopter mechanic in Vietnam who introduced the go-go girl to the district in 1969 when he opened up the Grand Prix Bar in Patpong: up to 1,756,000 men visited this bar between 1969 and 1981 (Rhodes, 1991: 69).

The turning point in the history of the sex service industry arrived when the Vietnam War ended. Hantrakul made a pointed observation regarding that critical moment:

> The withdrawal of the American forces from Vietnam led many people to expect that service industries which had grown up around the GI in Bangkok would immediately collapse, but this expectation turned out to be naive. The GI recreation patterns were overwhelmingly adopted by local clientele supported by the Thai permissive code of conduct for males. This local clientele continues to be important to the prostitution industry today (1988: 130).

---

[2] As Mies has pointed out:

> ...one should not forget the role played by so-called 'avant-garde or alternative' tourists, those who do not want to stay in big hotels but open up with their 'rucksack tourism', new areas and new fields for sexploitation. Often it was these avant-garde tourists and alternative travel guides who dared to break local and western taboos first, for example, by bathing naked on the beaches of Goa or by giving tips to tourists where to find still 'unpolluted, virgin land' for their hunger for sex and adventure. Whereas some years ago the authors of alternative travel guides to Asia would still admonish their customers to show respect for the culture of the local people and treat the women as human beings, many of them are now offering tips, usually received from globetrotters as to where to find the youngest and cheapest women in Asia. Their clients are the 'alternative' tourists, mostly young and with little money. But they are often the ones who create new needs and fashions (1989: 141).

However, besides the local clientele, tourist 'troops' have, especially since the late 1970s, replaced the American troops. For example, the number of tourists visiting Thailand rose from 212,000 in 1964 to 2,800,000 in 1986 (Ritcher, 1989: 85). This had increased even further to an estimated total of 5,000,000 in 1990, with estimated projections made by the Tourist Authority of Thailand that there would be at least 6,000,000 tourists in 1991 (*Bangkok Post*, 1990). The sex ratio of the tourist population was such that women were significantly outnumbered by men, at a ratio of 2 to 1, with the largest numbers being Japanese, German and Australian men (Rhodes, 1991: 65).

The sex tour operators justify their businesses by claiming that this is a new kind of development aid to the Third World. As one operator stated, the living conditions of people in the Bangkok slums made him cry all night, so he decided to organise sex tours to Thailand to help these women who were in distress (Skrobanek, 1990b: 11).

To attract clients, his as well as other agencies advertised in similar ways:

If you ever want to have an exclusive and special sex-holiday which you really will remember the rest of your life, then this is a unique opportunity.... Girls can be hired for a low price for a couple of hours, a whole night or a week.... You can get the feeling that taking a girl here is as easy as buying a package of cigarettes.... For the first time in history you can book a trip to Thailand with erotic pleasure included in the price (ibid).

Sick of women's rights fanatics? Join ScanThai. (Skrobanek, 1990c: 16)

Many clients return with 'once in a lifetime' memories. In a postcard thanking the sex tour company, David Gardiner, winner of the two-week Thailand holiday prize from the

Forum and Stag Tours Bangkok Holiday Competition, stated:

> [l]et me begin by saying that I had a terrific time.... It was more than just a romp in the sun – it was my first taste of a culture profoundly (not just superficially) different to my own, with very different attitudes to life, death, religion and sex; different notion of what is worth striving for in human existence.... The bar-girls were just as enchanting as I had been led to believe. To call them 'prostitutes' is to flatter the European practitioners of that trade – really a new word is needed. What they give is far more than sex – it includes friendship, tenderness, warmth – everything one might hope for from a 'girlfriend', even a rather idealized girl-friend. (Skrobanek, 1990b: 13).

Furthermore, after such experiences, it is not all that easy to return home to the West. Bryan Johnson, a former Asia correspondent for the *Globe and Mail*, and now an owner of a 'go-go' bar in Manila, confessed that:

> [w]hen I was back in Niagara last year I was stunned by the fact that girls ignored me – that checkout girls wouldn't make eye contact and flirt with me. It made me feel like I was dead, like a non-person, a ghost. It's a strange, eerie feeling to go back to that world (O'Malley, 1991: 88).

No doubt this is why those seeking 'happiness without frontiers' especially like Bangkok. As one German bar owner succinctly stated, 'It's the last place in the world where you can still be a white man' (Rhodes, 1991: 69).

In discussing sex tourism, it should be noted that its effects are not restricted to men visiting Thailand. There are, in addition, three by-products of sex tourism worth empha-sising: mail-order brides, traffic in women and international migration of Third-World women to countries of the First

World. For example, with respect to mail-order brides, the number of non-Thai men marrying Thai women has been steadily increasing. Such is the case in West Germany where, in 1986, 4,907 Thai women married West German men, compared to 4,371 in 1985 and 2,258 in 1980 (*The Nation*, 1989). Twenty West German companies were involved in the mail-order bride business. They conducted their businesses by placing advertisements in Thai newspapers, inviting interested women to send them their individual biographies, vital statistics and their photographs. The information provided by the women was then listed in catalogues for distribution to male clients. The women were then brought over to West Germany, for the men to make their selection. The clients had up to three months to make their final choice, in which time they could change a woman for a new one as many times as they wanted.

Many of these women have confessed that they not only had problems with the language, but also with their husbands' 'psychological disorderliness'. One woman recounted her experience of being ordered 'to put his shoe in my mouth and crawl on the floor while he was masturbating' (Skrobanek, quoted in Tantiwiramanond and Pandey, 1991: 110). A further problem was the manner in which they were regarded as 'goods' from which the men were determined to receive 'maximum benefit', even pushing them to prostitution in order to become profitable.

It is surprising to learn that, according to one government report, the traffic in women and young children mushroomed during 1976–82 without much response or concern from any of the enforcement agencies. Attracted by advertisements in the newspapers and direction persuasion from individual agents, many women go abroad by way of tour companies, employment agencies or marrying foreign tourists in the hope that there will be a better job with a high-paying salary in the new country (NCWA, 1991). However, it rarely turns out as expected.[3]

In the early part of this decade, the destination of most international migration of mail-order brides was Europe. Later, the mail-order bride business began to flourish in North America, and soon became a multi-million dollar industry across that continent (*Toronto Star*, 1991: A1, A8). There are several of these services operating in Canada, including Dateline in Ottawa, Calgary's Friendship Office and Toronto's Asian Connection. These businesses circulate catalogues with black and white photographs and short bio-blurbs listing the ages, measurements and weights of the women 'as coldly as used car magazines detail mileage and engine size' (ibid). Moreover, the Canadian police reported that Asian women are imported in groups of 20 to 30 to work in brothels disguised as health clubs or massage spas in malls and remote industrial plazas such as in the east end of Toronto. Soon after arriving, one 16-year-old Malaysian girl had to be treated in the hospital after the managers forced her to have intercourse with more than 40 clients in three days (*Macleans*, 1991).

Two other current issues which warrant special consideration are child prostitution and AIDS. It has been estimated that there are about 800,000 child prostitutes in Thailand.[4] Whereas

[3] This is another point that needs to be discussed. Naiyana Supapueng, the Co-ordinator of Friends of Workers in Asia (FOWIA), proposed that as most of these women know the situation but prefer to take the risk, the GOs' and NGOs' approach, in both exporting and importing countries, should be changed. They have to accept the truth of what is really going on and play more informative and supportive roles. (From Thammasat University's Women and Youth's Studies Programme's monthly round-table discussion on 'Female Migrant Labour', 26 July 1995).

[4] This number was proposed by the Centre for the Protection of Children's Rights. It seemed that Dr Kritaya Archavanitkul did not agree as she herself preferred the middle estimate. (See the early part of this chapter.)

Skrobanek suggested that the majority of clients are local men who believe that 'deflowering or sleeping with a very young or virgin girl will revitalise an old man's sexual potency' (1990a: 12), Kumprapan argued that this notion is a myth because 'when sex is intensely commercialised, consumers tend to look for more exotic, bizarre products. That's where child prostitution comes in' (quoted in Ekachai, 1990b: 25). Wasi, on the other hand, comments that foreign men 'have lots of money to spend, and this creates a heavy demand for prostitutes. And when the supply of young women falls short, the business goes to younger girls, leading to child prostitution' (ibid: 21).

When demand is greater than what is available locally, there is often an expansion of the sex trade into outlying areas in an effort to fulfil the need for new young prostitutes. Skrobanek observed that this often results in 'procuring children from various ethnic minorities, such as Akhas and Shans from Burma, and Laotians, for prostitution' (1990a: 12). Ekachai claims that many of the male prostitutes, who comprise an estimated 10 per cent of all child prostitutes in Thailand, are primarily 'runaway boys, the victims of domestic violence, neglect and rural development failure' (1990b: 23). Skrobanek adds that

> [t]heir numbers appear to be growing, especially among school boys in Bangkok and other big towns who have direct contact with tourists. But there are several rural villages in Northern Thailand where boys have become the prostitutes of well paying foreign visitors as well (1990a: 13).

In regard to the current AIDS situation in Thailand, there have been many studies undertaken by government agencies, NGOs and academics in an effort to determine the prevalence of the HIV virus. However, the statistics vary and are often under dispute. For instance, Erlanger criticised the WHO's conservative estimate that between 125,000 and 150,000 Thais will die from AIDS by 1997. Instead he is more in agreement with the Population and Community Development Association of Thailand who predict that the HIV virus could infect as many as 5.3 million by the year 2000, with more than a million dead by then. Currently, the epidemic is most advanced in Chiangmai, the most famous province in the North of Thailand. Erlanger reported further that up to 72 per cent of the prostitutes in Chiangmai's cheapest brothels carry the HIV virus (Erlanger, 1991: 26). He supports the opinion of Dr Vicharn Vithayasai, who said that

> we should keep these women in the brothels, where we can check them and teach them to use condoms. Otherwise, they will go underground and spread over the country, infecting many more… (ibid).

The situation of the increasing prevalence of the HIV virus among Thailand's population has reached a critical point. Jongsathitman, a researcher, even suggests that prostitution in the form of the rented wife could once again become the prevalent and private domain of the rich in their efforts to avoid the danger of HIV/AIDS that is so often associated with the general population of prostitutes (NCWA, 1991).

In addition to HIV/AIDS, militarism and its relation to prostitution continues to be an issue, especially in Third World countries. For example, although the Vietnam War has long been over, global militarism still plays a prominent role in Thailand's sex industry. The recent Gulf War provides an excellent example: our television sets tell us that the war is over – but it is not.

If we follow the soldiers from the battlefield in Iraq, we find that the war continues; only the form, content and place have changed. For example, soon after the war ended, the following situation was reported by Steven Erlanger from Pataya, the most popular beach in Southeast Thailand, near U-Tapao, which was the US airbase during the Vietnam War:

PATAYA, Thailand, March 24 The young women from Marilyn's A-GO-GO broke through the lines of staring tourists and hit the beach at about 11:30 this morning, and quickly formed an escort party for the 7,000 American sailors coming ashore here for their first liberty since victory in the Persian Gulf War.

Sharing the sand, somewhat uneasily, were about 400 wives and children, some with yellow ribbons and a few in yellow dresses, who had not seen their husbands since the aircraft carrier *Midway* and its battle group left for the Gulf on October 2.

Lieutenant J.G. Sherman Baldwin, a pilot from the Midway and the beach Duty officer, said: 'we're beating the men over the head to use condoms. The navy is doing all it can do in terms of information and education to get the word across to every 18 and 19-year-old sailor about how to protect themselves… (*The New York Times*, 1991).

This is an unrecognised part of the Gulf War, a part that took place in the Gulf of Thailand.

This is an overview of the prostitution problem in Thailand. However, what is needed is an in-depth analysis. For example, why have these girls become prostitutes? What has happened to them? What is really going on in a country that tries so hard to obtain the status of a 'developed' country?

All of these questions will be addressed in the remainder of this chapter through the discussion and review of several relevant books and articles. These literature sources include: *From Peasant Girls to Bangkok Masseuses* by Pasuk Phongpaichit (1982), 'Prostitution in Thailand' by Sukanya Hantrakul (1988), 'Tourism and the Price Women Pay' by Siriporn Skrobanek (1990b), and *Behind the Smile: Voices of Thailand* by Sanitsuda Ekachai (1990a). These four publications were chosen, firstly, because they were written in English and therefore are accessible to non-Thai readers. Furthermore, they were written by four Thai woman writers with different backgrounds and perspectives – a professor, a freelance writer, an activist and a journalist – at different times during the past decade. Their insightful studies will help provide an in-depth understanding of this problem from, what I hope to be, a Thai perspective.

Why have these girls become prostitutes? What would your choices be if you were born into a landless peasant family in a remote village in the poorest region of Thailand? Forests that were, at one time, your natural supermarket and pharmacy, have been converted into tourist resorts and eucalyptus plantations. Even though you may have some land left, the remoteness of the village has placed you 'at the end of the chain of rural marketing' (Phongpaichit, 1982: 42). Therefore, not only do you get poor prices for your products, you also suffer from the frequent fluctuations in demand. As Phongpaichit noted, many of the farmers in the North have complained that even when they took the risks of investing in new and commercial crops, they all too often found that the market was unreliable and the produce was difficult to sell (ibid).

What is the incentive for staying in your village when, by going to Bangkok, you can work in a factory and earn as much as 25 times what you could at home? (ibid: v). If you go into the sex trade, a couple of years of work would enable you to build a house for your family, of a size and quality which very few people in the countryside could ever hope to afford on the meagre earnings of a lifetime in agriculture (ibid: 74).

At this point, after having carried out in-depth interviews with 50 Bangkok masseuses, Phongpaichit came to the conclusion that

the economic incentive is patently clear. Most of the girls

came from the two poorest regions of the country (the North and the North-east), and chiefly from farming families with large numbers of dependents. Most of them had left because of the pressure of poverty (ibid: 14).

Before leaving home, most of the girls were either helping out on the family farm or were housewives. In addition, about 40 per cent of them had no formal education at all, while another 52 per cent had less than four years of elementary schooling (ibid: 12–14). In one study, the author points out that one of the most striking changes in the data on urban migration between 1960 and 1970 is that in the rural–urban movement from the Northeast to Bangkok, women exceeded men by a ratio of approximately 4:3, and in the rural–urban movement from the North to Bangkok, the ratio was 5:4. The study also indicates that the ages of the migrants were mostly concentrated in the group consisting of 15–24 year olds; furthermore, it is with the 10 to 19-year-old group that the number of women migrants exceeded the number of men. In conclusion, the study found that while on average only 44.4 per cent of the city's women (over the age of 11) participated in the labour force, the rate of participation by migrant women from the North was 54.5 per cent, and among migrant women from the Northeast it had soared up to 80.8 per cent (ibid: 32–5).

What is remarkable about these women who go to Bangkok, considering Thai attitudes toward women who allow more than one man access to her body, is that they manage to maintain strong ties with their families. They return home to visit at least once a year; in most cases it is often two or three times. Of 46 girls interviewed, all sent at least 1,000 baht (US$40) a month back home (ibid: 23). The postmaster in Dok Kam Tai district noted that the remittances swelled during the months of March to June and November to January. As the author noted,

[t]hese are the months of greatest activity in the agricultural calendar, and the girls increase their remittances to cover the costs of the wage labour which must be hired to sustain agricultural operations. Many of the families have had to replace their daughters' labour with hired help, and the daughters are aware of this substitution. If they have not made enough savings to send home for these seasonal needs, they may well turn up in person to do the necessary tasks. The migration is thus an adjunct to the family's (and thus the village's) agrarian economy (ibid: 69).

There are many studies on prostitution. Phongpaichit's study is unique, however, as it not only brings into focus the micro level, in particular, the socio-economic issues pertaining to Thai masseuses, but also brings into question the macro level – that is, the government economic development policies since 1950. Traditional development strategies, which promoted the accumulation of urban capital by utilising the surpluses of agriculture, have made Bangkok a rapidly growing primary city dominated by an urban middle class which monopolises wealth and political influence by 'squeezing' those who tend to be situated closer to the margins of the dominant society as they do not have the same social and geographical advantages. As the author concluded,

> … migration is thus an intrinsic part of Thailand's economic orientation. Thailand's strategy depends externally on accepting a dependent and vulnerable role in the world economy, and internally on keeping the primary sector in a dependent and tractable state. A business which takes girls out of the poorer parts of the countryside and sells their services to the urban earner and to the foreign visitor is merely the mirror image of this hierarchy of dependence (ibid: 75).

This kind of economic development can be characterised as

a *'penetration* of the global economy'. Additionally, the failure to adequately industrialise while trying to maintain their agricultural-based economy, caused Thailand to resort to earning foreign currency through the selling of 'nature and culture': i.e. sun, sand, sea, a sophisticated local way of life and, more importantly, the special service sector that promotes and sells sex to foreign tourists who normally cannot afford it in their own countries. Images of docility, submissiveness and the 'exotic' also play into the appeal of Thai prostitutes to foreign men.

Encouraged by the World Bank and other international funding agencies, this new policy has been promoted officially since 1980, which was declared the 'Year of Tourism'. Mr Boonchu Rojanasathien, the Deputy Prime Minister during that time, declared at the national governor's meeting in October 1980 that

> [w]ithin the next two years, we have a need of money. Therefore I ask of all governors to consider the natural scenery in your provinces, together with some forms of entertainment that some of you might consider disgusting and shameful because they are forms of sexual entertainment that attract tourists. Such forms of entertainment should not be prohibited if only because you are morally fastidious. Yet explicit obscenities that may lead to damaging moral consequences should be avoided, within a reasonable limit. We must do this because we have to consider the jobs that will be created for the people (quoted in Hantrakul, 1988: 130–1).

It is not only the ideology and practice of 'Western' capitalist patriarchy but also both traditional and contemporary 'Thai' patriarchy that make the problems of prostitution in Thailand more complicated. For example, a very unique characteristic of Thai prostitutes is that they continue to have a very close relationship with their families (while many prostitutes in the West are runaways who often no longer have any contact with their families).

There are many historical and cultural factors that have promoted the reduction of women to second-class citizens in Thai society.[5] For example, Hantrakul critically and concisely summarises that

> traditional Thai culture, partly rooted in the Buddhist concept of the accumulation of merit and the Law of Karma, encourages Thai women, particularly those living in rural areas, to view men as their superiors. Women see themselves as disadvantaged and less worthy. They need money as a means of showing gratitude to their parents for bearing and raising them, as a way of taking care of their younger siblings and giving them a wider range of opportunities, including education (Hantrakul, quoted in Tantiwiramanond and Pandey, 1991: 21).

Her comment reinforces an earlier study by Phongpaichit which stated that the most remarkable thing about the girls she interviewed was 'their conception of themselves as family breadwinners' (1982: 24). All but four retained strong links with their families, supplying remittances which contributed substantially to meeting the basic needs of their families for housing, water and education, but little to productive investment in rural areas (ibid: 23, v). For example, there is the story of Taew, a girl from the village of Don Barg in the Northeast, who was persuaded to sell her virginity at one of the massage

---

[5] This does not contradict what Aeusrivongse had stated earlier; that is, in terms of financial contributions, Thai women play a much more prominent role than men. However, politically, men have had superior status over women as their parents believe that it is the 'son' not 'daughter' who will bring a good reputation back to their families, through education and/or getting a good job (1994: 115).

parlours. The client paid 8,000 baht (US$200), of which she got only 2,000 baht (US$50). She sent the money home right away to build a well for drinking water (ibid: 52).

In conclusion, I feel that although both authors each explored different aspects of prostitution, with Phongpaichit focusing primarily on the economic element while Hantrakul explored the cultural background and viewpoints traditionally rooted in the doctrines and practices of Buddhism,[6] they nonetheless were able to reinforce and enrich each other's work.

However, their local and national accounts of the phenomenon of Thai prostitution would remain wholly incomplete without considering the international dimension. In this respect, Siriporn Skrobanek's article 'Tourism and the Price Women Pay' remains invaluable. In this article, Skrobanek, who is the founder of the Foundation For Women, clearly addresses and analyses international phenomena of packaged sex tours, mail-order brides and the overall global traffic in women. From all three perspectives, one can easily develop the broader context in which to better understand why someone like Taew, a virgin peasant girl from the remote village of Don Barg in the Northeast, would want to migrate to Bangkok to become a masseuse and later end up in the Hamburg, Frankfurt or Amsterdam red-light district through the mail-order bride business or other channels. Phongpaichit, describing this phenomenon from the local and national levels, says that these peasant girls

… were not fleeing from a family background or rural society which oppressed women in conventional ways.

---

[6] This point needs to be discussed in depth and breadth. Many would agree that to take advantage of women or to place them in the inferior status is not the essence of Buddha's teaching. Buddhism is a religion that encourages people to think intellectually, not to believe blindly.

Rather, they were engaging in an entrepreneurial move designed to sustain the family units of a rural economy which was coming under increasing pressure. They did so because their accustomed position in that rural society allocated to them a considerable responsibility for earning income to sustain the family (ibid: vi).

From the rural countryside to urban Bangkok, these girls were later attracted, through various newspaper ads and agents promising high-paying jobs, to the major urban centres of the world, especially in Europe and North America; in this way, they made a second periphery-to-centre migration.

This particular phenomenon of the international migration of Thai prostitutes is given further support by Enloe, who claims that

[t]he International Monetary Fund, which serves as a vanguard for the commercial banking community by pressuring indebted governments to adopt policies which will maximize a country's ability to repay its outstanding loans with interest, has insisted that governments cut their social-service budgets. Reductions in food-price subsidies are high on the IMF's list of demands for any government that wants its financial assistance. Keeping wages down, cutting back public works, reducing the number of government employees, rolling back health and education budgets – these are standard IMF prescriptions for indebted governments. They usually attract support from at least some members of the government itself, especially in the financial ministry (1989: 184).

Therefore, when a woman from Mexico, Jamaica or the Philippines decides to emigrate in order to make money as a domestic servant 'she is designing her own international debt policies. She is trying to cope with the loss of earning power and the rise in the cost of living at home by cleaning bathrooms in the country of the bankers' (ibid: 85).

This analysis is also relevant to the case of the international migration of Thai prostitutes. For example, when Ning, a nightclub bar-girl in Bangkok, decided to follow Robert Meier, a Swiss tourist, to Zurich, she had developed her own international economic policy with the intention of supporting her family; but she had done so without knowing that she would be forced to work as a prostitute in Zurich, as well as in Paris where her husband would sometimes take her (Gabriel-Luzon, 1987: 2). This reinforces what Phongpaichit had also discovered:

> The trade has been successfully oriented to an urban and international market and embedded deeply into the structure of Thai economy. It provides a means of survival for poor and rural families, and it helps earn the foreign exchange to cover import costs (1982: 75).

By critically reading the work of these authors, which tend to complement and support each other, I have gained a clearer understanding of the problems of prostitution in Thailand within a global context. I can now answer my questions step-by-step: Why prostitution? Because of global militarism and economics.[7] Why global militarism and economics? Because

---

[7] Of course, I value that the local cultural factors are also the causes of this phenomenon. However, this study was done while I was away from home. As a Thai woman travelling abroad, my passport always got checked thoroughly by the immigration officers at the airports in many countries. I was looked at strangely and treated differently from other travellers. As a Thai student at school, I was tired of answering the questions about Bangkok, bars and child prostitutes, etc. In an effort to understand the situation of my 'Third World' homeland while locating myself in the centre of a First World country, I found that I had to put a 'local' fragment in the 'global' frame to perceive the whole picture. Therefore, the table should be turned around to those questioners: they have to question themselves, not just us. Additionally, I began writing this chapter in 1991, the first year of

global consumerism and tourism play a big role in that process. As Mies points out, '... the prevailing world market system, oriented toward unending growth and profit, cannot be maintained unless it can exploit external and internal colonies: nature, women and other people' (1991: 8).

Consumption patterns are becoming more and more complicated. For example, it is because of the surplus produced in the South that people in the North now have more time and more money for leisure activities and material goods. Leisure time activity no longer only means sports or travelling; it also includes exotic sexual consumption as well.

However, the data strongly suggests that in Thailand it is the Thai men who are the major clients of the prostitutes. In Western countries, only men considered to be 'losers' go to prostitutes, but in Thailand to go to a prostitute seems to be as acceptable as any other common activity, such as going to a party, seeing a movie or playing sports. Hantrakul makes a very interesting observation regarding this point. She says that

[c]ulturally Thai society still very much flatters men for their promiscuity and polygamy.... While a woman is seriously condemned for allowing more than one man to gain access to her body, a man is, ironically, praised for being able to, on whatever basis – love, money or even force – have sexual relations with as many women as he wishes (1988: 117, 132).

[7] (cont.) my study in a Canadian university. From then to now, six years have passed by and there have been so many critical studies on this issue. For example, some no longer consider women who enter into this job as 'victims' but the 'actors' who maturely choose their own way of living. Therefore these new ideas make this chapter, written in 1991–94, become a historical piece. The change in the stream of thought regarding this issue in each time-period is very interesting. However, the most exciting one should be the study of prostitution by prostitutes themselves.

Therefore, even if the number of foreign customers were to decrease significantly, the occurrence of prostitution in Thai society would remain strong as it has been acceptable and available as an everyday activity of Thai male culture. As Hantrakul further explains,

> [i]n Thai family life the major point of conflict in marriage stems from the fear of minor wives. This fear and subsequent marital conflict, together with financial predicaments, has led to many women preferring their husbands to visit prostitutes rather than to take a second or minor wife.... For virtuous young Thai virgins, the prostitute is a necessity, providing an opportunity for their male lovers to gain experience before they marry. For loving mothers, the prostitute is an adventure, a social service, a cultural universal for males.... Outside the family there are several social workers who, whenever there is an increase in the incidence of rape, stress the necessity of promoting prostitution as if that were the answer in a society where there is already easy access to prostitutes (ibid: 133).

Above all, I do agree with her insightful comment that the general attitude of the Thai prostitute, that is, 'her fatalistic acceptance of her profession combined with her feudalistic sense of rendering service to her superiors and her self-taught art of commercialism' (ibid: 134), has contributed to the acceptability and availability of prostitution in Thailand compared to her sisters in other countries.

In addition to Thailand's traditional patriarchy, which has oppressed Thai women for hundreds of years, the patriarchy of Western capitalism, which articulates itself under the name of 'development', has 'squeezed' and 'pushed' them even further toward the periphery of Thai socio-economic culture. The effect of this double oppression is, as Shiva argues, that development itself is the problem as it drains resources away from those who need them the most, therefore pushing them ever more into the margins:

> ... what is currently called development is essentially maldevelopment, based on the introduction or accentuation of the domination of man over nature and women.... Nature and women are turned into passive objects, to be used and exploited for the uncontrolled and uncontrollable desires of alienated man. From being the creators and sustainers of life, nature and women are reduced to being 'resources' in the fragmented, anti-life model of mal-development (1990: 6).

In the case of Thailand, it cannot be denied that develop-ment, under the many different labels of industrialisation, modernisation, exportation, etc., has been the primary contri-butor of ecological dysfunction and environmental degrada-tion. For example, in the Northeastern region it has been found that

> [a] contributing factor to erratic and fewer rainfalls has been the clearing of the tropical forest over the past two to three decades to grow cash crops such as maize, tobacco and tapi-oca which is mainly sold to the animal feed markets of the European Economic Community. The loss of the forest has also caused soil erosion, lowering the quality and fertility of the land still further (Ekachai, 1990a: 20).

In the overall region, the percentage of forest to total land area has dropped sharply from 53.1 per cent in 1967 to 29.1 per cent in 1985. What's more, it has been estimated that 'most if not all of the forests of Thailand will disappear permanently in the next three decades, unless very drastic measures are taken to stop the current trend' (Ramitanondh, 1989: 27, 31).

This critical situation has affected women even further by marginalising them, thereby placing them in an increasingly desperate position. As Shiva explains,

[w]hen commodity production as the prime economic activity is introduced as development, it destroys the potential of nature and women to produce life and goods and services for basic needs. More commodities and more cash means less life – in nature (through ecological destruction) and in society (through denial of basic needs). Women are devalued first because their work cooperates with nature's processes, and second, because work which satisfies needs and ensures sustenance is devalued in general.... It is no accident that the modern, efficient and productive technologies created within the context of growth in market economic terms are associated with heavy costs, borne largely by women (Shiva, 1990: 7).

Shiva's observations are very pertinent to the situation in Thailand for it appears that Thai women have been affected the most by development. For example, a recent study by the Gender and Development Research Institute (1991) indicates that the Thai female labour force in the agricultural sector has significantly decreased from 87.6 per cent to 57.5 per cent over the last two decades (1970–88). In addition, from 1985–88, female labourers migrating to the urban areas outnumbered migrating male labourers by a total of two million. Most of them were among the 15–24 age group and were serving as the primary labour force in the textile, garment, shoe, food processing, electronic equipment and tourism industries. The rest earned very low wages in the informal sector such as domestic work, street vending. Later, it would be no surprise to learn that many end up in prostitution in order to earn more wages.

Through the critique of development, the flip side being consumerism, we can gain a clearer understanding of the roots of poverty and prostitution in Thailand. This is reinforced by Ekachai's recent work, *Behind the Smile*, which sharply reflects this phenomenon. The writer travelled from village to village in the three major regions of Thailand and heard first-hand what rural people had to say. She recorded the changing face of Thailand from the perspective of rural Thai villagers. These stories are insightful in their depiction of the radical changes occurring in Thailand over these past three decades: from an agricultural society to an industrialised and modernised one. For example, Wan Tankhiaw, a woman from the Lua tribe in the North of Thailand, recalled that

> [s]ince the school was set up, we have no longer worn our traditional clothes ... other people used to look at us as if we were freaks. We want to dress like them (Ekachai, 1990a: 177).

The author tells us further that there are now only two pieces of traditional, hand-woven Lua cloth, dating back over three generations, left in the village. This situation is made worse by the fact that none of the young girls today know how to weave (ibid: 834).

This is what has been occurring as a result of the government establishing an agricultural centre, which later became a school and Buddhist temple, with the goal to 'assimilate' hilltribe people into the modern age and to 'persuade' them to give up their old so-called 'uncivilised' ways.

Not surprisingly, these changes that have swept through the hilltribe community have been predominantly for the worse. For example, Ekachai reiterates the experience of Wan's brother's family. After getting caught cutting down forest trees illegally, Wan's brother had to leave his wife, Moon, and four children in order to serve out a seven-year prison sentence. Soon after, in order to support the family, Moon's eldest daughter was 'sold' to a brothel. As much as we may feel inclined to judge Moon, we need first to understand the economic desperation that this family is experiencing, caused by forces and institutions far beyond their control.

Moon is distraught over the loss of her husband and daughter. She says:

> I miss my child. I miss my husband. You don't know how I suffer. I feel helpless trying to make ends meet, struggling on my own. You don't know what it's like.... I didn't sell my child.... I just borrowed money.... That's why I only asked her boss for 2,000 baht (US $50). That's all I needed to buy rice and food. They offered 10,000 baht (US $250) for her. But I didn't want her to have to work too long to pay off the debt. I wanted her to come back home (ibid: 179, 175).

By not only relying on theory but also grounding this in the oral and experiential testimony of local rural people, Ekachai's work is both creative and critical. However, by doing so, she not only brings the unheard voices of marginalised people to the 'centre' but also challenges the centre through these 'real-life stories' of the unheard voices. For example, in her chapter 'Invasion of the North', she critically addresses current development policies:

> Government and private-sector promotion of cash crops, which require a high investment, is decreasing the capabilities of small farmers for self-reliance and self-sufficiency in food [production]. The increasing use of chemical pesticides is affecting the environment's soil and health of the farmers (ibid: 126–7).

Moreover, what makes her work unique is her ability to take several perspectives into account. The stories that she presents reflect her 'excellent understanding of the complex and interwoven human, social and ecological issues involved, and her ability to communicate this' (ibid: 13). I do agree with her observation that the traditional way of life has become somewhat 'diluted as the villagers are engulfed by the market economy, land speculation and tourism. Rural communities are gradually losing their unique cultural heritages and their sense of identity' (ibid: 127). Moreover, the recent phenomenon of the increasing need for money for material consumption has deeply shaped the faces of the villages:

> Rural people have developed a high demand for motor-cycles, consumer appliances such as televisions and refrigerators, and other consumer goods. The rapid spread of good roads and electricity throughout the regions has brought city life and consumer culture, continuously promoted through the mass media, into their homes. As agricultural income alone is not sufficient to buy these goods, the village youth leave for the cities to look for extra earnings (ibid: 128).

The accumulating debt crisis has a double-bind relation with modern technology and its derivative, agribusiness. In the wake of decreasing self-sufficiency, youths are pushed to go to Bangkok in an effort to find employment, which in most circumstances remains scarce. As a result, the increasing demand for and the higher pay earnings of prostitutes has made prostitution a more popular alternative for many women in certain areas of the Northern region; that is, '[i]t has become a major source of income and the "key to survival" in the modern era' (ibid).

Although I started off explaining that prostitution had become a primary source for earning the extra income necessary for maintaining the basic needs of the poor, this appears to be changing as an increasing number of women are turning to prostitution to earn money for the acquisition of luxury consumer goods. What is the reality? Both processes are parts of neo-colonialist phenomenon. On the one hand, the subsistence farmers are starved out and their daughters necessarily become prostitutes in order to survive;[8] on the other hand, we cannot deny that, by embracing a consumer culture, Thai culture has become devalued. Thai people need to be like Westerners now, as well. The consumerist, imperialist culture of the North, which has been injected through media and market mechanisms, has ruined urban and rural Southern communities in many different ways, and to different degrees. In the rural areas, in some families, sisters follow each other, one after another, into the brothels. In the cities, one can find many different kinds of member clubs which can supply their customers with 'high class' escorts who work as secretaries, sales girls, or even students during the day, and work at night to earn extra money so that they can acquire those luxury consumer goods that reflect an increasingly desirable modern lifestyle.

But let's go back to Ekachai's work. I found that even though her report depicts the hardships of a struggling people, who are barely able to survive and meet their daily needs, it is still full of hope and liveliness. As she pointed out, 'some farmers are turning to integrated farming, which is based on principles of ecological balance and self-reliance, producing food for their own consumption before food for sale' (ibid: 127). This is perhaps what is most charming about this book: it not only confronts bitter problems but also provides a glimmer of hope for possible solutions to these seemingly intractable problems. There is an expectation of change for the better, as experienced by the author herself:

> as a result of her visits and conversations with so many villagers, she has come to respect their sound wisdom, wisdom which may itself provide answers to the many

---

[8] This statement might be disagreeable. Actually, prostitution is not the only means to survive. There are many forms of alternative work. However, it seems that this is the most effective way of earning a large sum of money in a short period of time.

problems Thailand faces, if we only listen to it (ibid: 13).

In conclusion, I'd like to say that these four books and articles make a tremendous contribution in helping us understand the problems of and associated with prostitution in Thailand. In working from differing perspectives, they help enrich and support each other. Phongpaichit (1982) began by exploring from an economic perspective under the theme of periphery–centre migration. What she found was that 'the girls did not make the economic structure, and they could not escape from it' (ibid: vi). Therefore, if there is to be a realistic solution to this crisis, it must be long-term, that is, 'a massive change in the distribution of income between city and countryside and a fundamental shift in Thailand's orientation to the international economy' (ibid: 76). Hantrakul's (1988) questioning of Thai patriarchal values was extremely pro-vocative and challenging. She also clearly outlined a proposal for the 'radical examination and change in the sexual relations between women and men both within and outside the institution of prostitution itself' (ibid: 135). Skrobanek (1990b) has brought her research on the transnational sexual exploitation of Thai women into the community, and brought the community back into the international forum, through her own established NGO, Foundation For Women (FFW) which aims at helping women in distress.[9] Ekachai's two articles, 'Go South, Young Girl' and 'I Didn't Sell My Daughter' utilised an environmental and holistic approach in her critique of global industrialisation and modernisation. She synthesises the various socio-economic, political and ecological backgrounds

[9] Another recent step in moving toward solving this critical problem is the establishment of the Global Alliance Against Traffic in Women (GAATW) at the International Workshop on Migration and Traffic in Women which was held in Thailand in October 1994. The aim of GAATW is 'not to stop the migration of women but to ensure the human rights of those who are trafficked' (FFW, 1995:1).

which help bring into focus the work of all four authors.

The process of development has managed to undermine the self-sufficiency of the rural economy, thereby pushing those like Doaw, a farm girl, to strategically re-adjust and find new sources of income for her and her family's survival by doing erotic shows and selling her body to both local and foreign men. It has also pushed many female workers at the Bic pen factory to work like machines, as they have to endlessly repeat the same gestures to 'assemble more than a hundred thousand ballpoint pens per day' (Nelson, 1989: 97).

However, the term 'development' in general and the strategy of 'integrating women into development' in particular, means something different to me, a well-educated middle-class Thai woman.

First of all, like many other women in the North, I am able to buy cheap Bic pens (only US$0.08 or 3 baht in Bangkok) and a variety of cheap commodities all year round. Secondly, it allows me the opportunity to climb up the education ladder and upgrade myself by getting a scholarship provided by the 'Women in Development Consortium in Thailand' (WIDCIT) to come to study in a First World country like Canada. Consequently, it also means that I have a chance to take the 'Women and Development' course and do research on issues relevant to the female factory workers and prostitutes in Thailand.

I have on my desk many letters of invitation from academic institutions in North America, airplane ticket receipts and honorarium cheques. During the past few years, I have earned hundreds of dollars for giving lectures on this sensational and 'sexy' topic. The farther I fly, the clearer I see what I have heard or read:

Is development cornucopia or catastrophe? Development has brought industrialisation, environmental destruction, agribusiness and militarism to the South. Southern development, meanwhile, has brought immense prosperity to the North, by creating and reinforcing neocolonist economic relationships and consumerism. It has also created an immense development industry in the North, whereby Northern academics enjoy lucrative careers as development 'experts'. *The hegemonic view of development held by the North, therefore, is very self-serving.*

Finally, I have realised bit by bit that the meaning of 'development' is something more complicated than can be explained by using only a political economy approach. Integrating 'women' into 'development' doesn't refer only to 'those' women in the four major sectors,[10] i.e. factory workers, informal sector workers, agricultural workers, and sex service workers, who have been integrated into the global market system; it also includes me.

In the exclusive domain of the university, I have had a chance to make 'links' with other women who are struggling in the 'pores' of capitalism, not by working side by side in the factory or brothel, but by studying and researching 'about' them. Is academia the privileged place of locating oneself in the (invisible) centre, therefore taking up a legitimising power in the process of naming and objectifying the 'others' (by naming it 'knowledge')? What remains even more problematic is that through this type of 'self-serving/centralising and objectifying of the other', a necessary part of the development process, I have even excluded both the experience of my own roots and of my own mother as 'the other'.

---

[10] Generally, it is understood that the economic system is divided into tri-sectors: industry, agriculture and service. However, in terms of integrating 'women as housewives into the capitalist accumulation process', Mies has analysed that it takes place in four major areas as mentioned above (1989: 114–5).

Let them come and see men and women and children who know how to live, whose joy has not yet been killed by those who claimed to teach other nations how to live.

CHINUA ACHEBE

5

What Does 'Development' Mean to *My Mother?*

This is my 75-year-old mother. She has never applied for a job in her life. She has never had a résumé. If she was to have one, she would probably write a short one-sentence résumé: a housewife for 58 years.

Love my mother,
love her plants.

My mother was born in 1916 in a remote village in the south of Thailand. She finished grade 3 around 1925–6 and went to work on her grandparents' farm. On 3 November 1933 she got married and had her first child a year later; five more soon followed.

After her husband passed away, she doesn't have to do much 'housewife' work. All her children are now grown up, a number of whom have given her ten grandchildren in all. At the age of 75, she spends most of her time in and out of her garden which is also her in-house pharmacy.

Four years ago, I would never have thought that I would be asking my mother what development means to her nor that I would be relating her life experiences to any of the aspects discussed in the 'Women and Development' course I had taken in the Winter term of 1991. From the perspective of

With her bamboo tree.

Making her 'green' rulers and pins from bamboo tree.

Gathering mangoes with a fruit-picker she made from bamboo tree.

Mango is a precious gift of summer. We wait for the whole year to see it and eat it.

Peeling her mangoes.

Using her home-made rake.

mainstream development concept, the phrase 'Women and Development' seems to implicitly refer to 'oppressed women in the poor countries'. However, my mother is no longer poor. She no longer has to work as a fruitpicker in the forest (at a time when black bears were commonly encountered there), to make and sell biscuits, nor to cut rice in the harvest season, etc. in order to earn a few extra baht for her family. After over fifty years of struggling, she is now an elderly middle-class woman who has her own house and her own garden to work in.

At that time a few years ago, I did not come across any challenging ideas that would allow me to critically place her in the 'development' context. Therefore, when I had to give a presentation and write a term paper as a course requirement, I unhesitatingly chose to do research on the most marginalised (but highly attractive academically) group of Thai women, that is, prostitutes, instead.

My four Canadian (read: white) classmates, who were granted scholarships to do their 'field work' in Indonesia, gave presentations on the topic of the Indonesian women's movement from a variety of perspectives, such as medical, political and historical. Another two, who were about to leave for Kenya, brought up the issues of African and refugee women.

Officially, there are no regulations to prevent me from exploring Canadian or any other ethnic groups. However, like many other 'international students' who received scholarships from development projects, it implicitly seemed that we 'should' focus on our own issues in our own homes. That is the way it is. At that moment, I did not question as to why a Thai student had to focus on Thai issues, while Canadian students had much more academic privilege and freedom to study and speak about any women's issues in any continent from around the world. It was not until I came across post-colonial feminist writings such as Trinh T. Minhha's *Women, Native, Other*, that I began to open my eyes to the new boundary discourses of post-colonial critique. Her critique can be metaphorically and powerfully applied to the development ideology (which has its roots in anthropological discourse) when she argues that Western anthropology is

> ...'a conversation of man with man'. Simplicity, however, has its own exactingness, and the questions immediately raised here will be: What 'man' and which 'man'? It seems clear that the favourite object of anthropological study is not just *any* man but a specific kind of man: the Primitive, now elevated to the rank of the full yet needy man, the Native.... The 'conversation of man with man' is, therefore, mainly a conversation of 'us' with 'us' about 'them', of the white man with the white man about the primitive-native man.
>
> A conversation of 'us' with 'us' about 'them' is a conversation in which 'them' is silenced. 'Them' always stands on the other side of the hill, naked and speechless, barely present in its absence. Subject of discussion, 'them' is only admitted among 'us', the discussing subjects, when accompanied or introduced by an 'us' member, hence the dependency of 'them' and its need to acquire good manners for the membership standing. The privilege to sit at the table with 'us', however, proves both uplifting and demeaning. It impels 'them' to partake in the reduction of itself and the appropriation of its otherness by a detached 'us' discourse.... Anthropology is finally better defined as 'gossip' (we speak together about others) than as 'conversation' (we discuss a question), a definition that dates back to Aristotle (1989: 64–8).

I would not have been able to appreciate this critical piece of post-colonial writing had I not also undergone a similar experience of finding myself in that post-colonial 'in-between' space of 'First World/Third World'; of 'us and them'. That is, the process of critical learning regarding the concept of 'development' which had taken place during my daily struggles and experiences as one of the 'others', i.e. as

A coconut tree.

My mother can make many kinds of toys and tools from this tree.

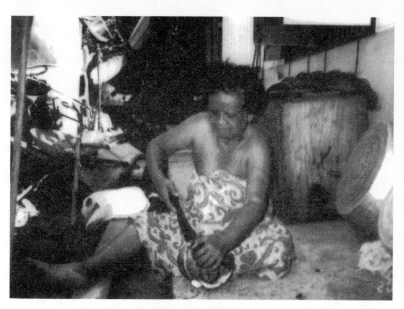

Peeling her coconut.

Making coconut milk for curry.

occupying one of several different labels, such as 'Third World' student or 'Woman of Colour'. Above all, it has provided me with a unique opportunity to do a timely oral environmental and historical dialogue with my own mother which became a part of my final project for the courses 'Environmental Education' and 'Photography for Social Change'.

That was the way it started. It was not 'once upon a time...'; it was the first Wednesday of March in the winter of the year 1991:

> ... my classmates and I had a deep and broad discussion on the topic of environmental education curriculum. As the only student from Thailand in the class, I was surprised to see that many of the colourful curriculum guidebooks provided for Canadian students were designed *to teach the children here how to touch, to hug and to kiss the trees.*

A horse and a gun – hand-made nature toys from banana trees.

Why is this subject and activity being taught?

What is wrong with the relationship between nature and human beings here?

This is something very strange and unusual compared to my own experiences. I have grown up with nature always around me. At my house in Bangkok, just stepping into the backyard I can pick up any kind of fruit I like: papaya, mango, jackfruit, guava, banana, sugar apple and rose apple, etc. It is my mother's place. It is because of her that I still experience nature as alive inside me.

'Banana trees need burning soil and green grass as fertilizer.' That is what she had learned from her grandfather. Her plump and healthy banana trees are growing day by day,

123

A planting tip: banana trees like recently burnt soil and freshly cut green grass.

(*Drawing by Ann S. Walker,*
International Women's Tribune Centre)

night by night. What a tree of life! My mother never buys aluminum foil or plastic wrap. She uses banana leaves and string made from the dried banana trunk. There have also been many different kinds of nature toys that she had made for me from the banana tree when I was young.

Her other magic plants are bamboo and coconut. We use bamboo shoots and coconut milk for cooking. My mother also makes rulers, rakes, brooms, and fruit picking instruments from these plants. The burning of the coconut husk acts as a natural insect repellent that helps keep mosquitoes away.

Next, let's see what she has in her kitchen garden: lemon grass, basil, ginger, galingale, chili and pumpkin, etc. These

Instead of aluminium foil or plastic wrap, my mother uses banana leaves.

Peeling a banana tree trunk to make banana string (left). Banana string being used with a banana leaf wrapper (below).

herbs are not only used as ingredients in cooking but also as multi-purpose in-house medicines; for example, lime and salt for coughs and sore throats and tamarind leaves and red onions placed in boiling water to be used as a cold remedy.

Her prescription for a cold: a handful of tamarind leaves, some red onions, and boiling water.
Direction: Inhale and exhale the steam, take a bath and put the concoction on your head.

(Drawing by Ann S. Walker, International Women's Tribune Centre)

These are her natural products: a mop-handle and a rake made of bamboo. A broom made from dried coconut leaves is on the left.

There is no need to pay for fuel as she often uses her in-house energy resources. Bit by bit, piece by piece, my mother collects old bamboo branches, rotten wood and coconut shells to use as her fuel wood.

The light wood, which produces heavy smoke, is used to start the fire. Later, the hard wood is put in as the main firewood. Note: The copper rice cooker on the stove is 58 years old!

While the rice is boiling, she is able to do other things. Often housework involves doing two or three jobs at the same time. When doing dishes there is no need for dishwashing liquid and scrub pads. The coconut husk and ash (in a small coconut-shell container – can you see it?) serve as her natural dishwashing utilities.

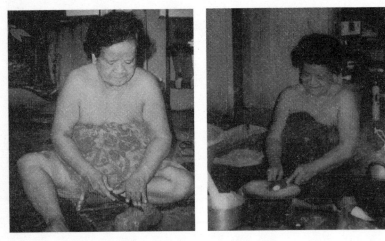

Sometimes while the rice is boiling she sharpens her knives ... or cuts bamboo shoots for making soup.

She dries her fish and chili in the sun and during the rainy season she stores rain water in jars for drinking.

My mother saw a bowling game on TV. She then created her own bowling ball and pins by using a coconut and several empty beer bottles.

How many plastic bags did you use during these past ten years? It was around 3,650 bags, if you used 1 per day. My mother has sustainable bags.... Look at her basket collection.... The biggest one on the left has been used for almost 10 years.

It is ironic that after travelling 10,000 miles to study many new environmental subjects with many new technical terms (such as reduce-reuse-recycle, sustainable development, resource management, energy conservation, indigenous knowledge and ecofeminism), that all along this new knowledge had already been taught to me, at a practical level, year by year, by my Mother (Sitthiraksa, 1993: 22–3).

Rethinking my mother's life story within the context of 'development' has emphasised for me that the latter is primarily for the sake of consumption in the North (of course, I don't deny that there is a 'North' in the South too) and can maintain itself only by first pushing the self-sufficient, environmentally sound and unconsumptive lifestyle of local rural people to the margins. It therefore has reinforced for me what I had learned from Verhelst:

… indigenous cultures are more than just obstacles to a development that tries to impose cultural alienation. They are also economic, social and political sources of life….

130

Too often the values of the Third World are irredeemably damaged by models of social change based on consumption, competition, acquisition and on the manipulation of human aspirations (1990: 22–3, 19).

It is said, 'if you educate a man, you educate a person; if you educate a woman, you educate the whole family'. Her long-lived teaching tool, a slate, was used and reused and reused again and again from her first to her sixth child.

My mother's story has taught me that the Western lifestyle of consumption is not the 'only' way to live, but that there are many alternative paths to walk. However, they have been suppressed, devalued, delegitimised and marginalised. This leads me to understand a third meaning of development; that it is *the process of imposing Western knowledge which requires the eradication of indigenous knowledge*. At this point, Vachon, quoted by Verhelst, concludes that '"developers" do not really acknowledge that each people might have ... a technical, socio-economic and juridico-political culture which is peculiar to them and which is wrong to suppress, even in the name of development' (ibid: 18). As he continues to elaborate,

our sanctimonious missions of civilisation, development, conscientisation, modernisation, social change, democratisation, liberation, social justice, and even of cooperation and international solidarity, are often Trojan horses *vis-a-vis* the traditions of Africa, Asia and the Americas. It is in this sense that, in the name of literacy, the oral traditions of the local people are destroyed; in the name of agricultural reform, of the best distribution of the land, wages and full employment, we destroy their original, non-monetary economic culture which is bound in a cooperative partnership with Mother Earth; in the name of our democracies we destroy their *dharma*-cracies; in the name of the acquisition of national sovereignty and the Nation State, we destroy their anti-state organisations; in the name of democratic taking of power, we destroy their original consensual political culture of leaders without power; that finally, in the name of human rights, we destroy their traditional judicial world which sees man not as a subject of rights but primarily as a subject of acts of grace, of gratitude and cosmic responsibility. Certainly, we must make people aware of the structures of dependence and of the external domination exercised by multinationals and governments. But the heart of the problem will remain untouched unless we are aware of the network of internal dependence and domination exercised by modern Western culture itself. Indeed, the dominating factor is not primarily the multinationals, national and international governments or even capitalist, Marxist or socialist ideologies, but our modern Western culture itself. And our international solidarity and cooperation movements are often, unconsciously, its first more or less voluntary slaves and its first more or less conscious ambassadors abroad (ibid).

I wish she would let me write her résumé. If I could I would list her experiences as follows: gardener, agriculturalist, cook, entertainer, tool and toy inventor and maker, traditional doctor, resources manager, energy conservationist, food scientist, home economist teacher, sustainable developer, ecologist and ... environmentalist.

Frankly, I'm very tired of having other women interpret for
us, other women sympathise with us. I'm interested in
articulating our own directions, our own aspirations, our
own past, in our own words. …At the same time I want to
tell our own young women that we don't need to grow up
wanting to be like 'Dick And Jane'. I want them to know that
it is not only all right, it's *necessary* for us to grow up in a
way that we have articulated ourselves: we don't need
governments, laws, or legislative frameworks to articulate
the whole concept of self-government and self-direction.

SKONAGANLEH: RÁ

6

What Does 'Development' Mean to Me?

She is my first environmental education teacher who taught me the concepts and practices of environmental education through her unwritten environmental education curriculum (Sitthiraksa, 1993: 23).

Inquiring into my mother's life helped me make critical connections between the theoretical and practical issues related to the environment and development. It is she who provided me with a living curriculum which she did not have to objectify by writing it down into a chapter format – she is already doing it day by day. My mother doesn't speak the jargon that has become popular in everyday modern life, such as 'conservation', 'sustainable development', 'ecofeminism' and 'waste management'. She doesn't busy herself filling blue boxes or wearing a 'Reduce-Reuse-Recycle' button, for she has been doing it all her life for over 75 years, including the additional motto … 'Refuse'. She refuses the unhealthy consumerist lifestyle that has been damaging much of Thailand's environment. (In this sense I don't mean to say that my mother resists change but neither does she want to totally discard Thai tradition. She enjoys listening to Buddhist radio programmes and watching debates on TV, daily.)

It seems that there is so much to learn from my own 'ground'. However, I don't mean a 'fixed' space left behind where I can return to. My own ground is the nurturing sources that facilitate the ongoing critique of, or dialogue with, the fixed and privileged ground of Western development. My mother has been, and continues to be, a simple and humble environmentalist for over three-quarters of a century. Why did I ignore her for such a long time? Why does her voice remain unheard? Why do so few people listen to her? Why have I just begun to revalue both my own earlier experiences and my mother's experiences? Why have these perspectives and real life stories been excluded from formal education and development discourse?

Again, why did I ignore my mother for such a long time? First of all, I was born in Thailand during the critical period which is the so-called 'Dawn of Development'. Some were born in the year 1955, when the Thai Television company began broadcasting under the auspices of Radio Corporation of America (RCA). A few years later in 1959, the World Bank Survey Mission Group came to Thailand and published its report entitled *A Public Development Program for Thailand*. It is said that this report 'was not only a critique of Thailand's previous performance in political economic development but was also a blueprint for Thailand's postwar development practices' (Charoensin-o-larn, 1988: 4). Many were born in 1960, which was the founding year for the Tourism Authority of Thailand. Since then, many of us have witnessed, in all regions of the country, the large-scale clearcutting of the rainforests, to make way for several hydro-electric dams.

It seems that my generation is historically situated in that 'in-between' place where we have experienced the tension between Westernisation (i.e. modernity) and Thai tradition. Through the lens of modernity, we can see only the (so-called) 'bright' side of development. From that moment onwards, we were no longer sure of who we were.

Secondly, through the process of dialoguing with my mother, I found that being socialised into the mainstream educational system during the 'development era' had alienated me from my own mother. What is worse is that I had misunderstood her; to me, she was just another old-fashioned, rural woman. I felt ashamed of my own roots. To be unmodern (read: unWestern) was not acceptable. I felt so embarrassed, as a child, to use my mother's home-made and hand-made bamboo ruler at school, instead of the plastic rulers others were using. At that time, who dared to be unmodern? Who dared challenge 'the universal code of dominant culture which denies the existence of difference?' (Long, 1993: 48).

After the imposition of several decades of Western develop-ment on Thai society, our traditional values and knowledge have become marginalised. How often in my life have I heard my mother recall ecological tips taught to her by her grandfather (my mother had been orphaned as a little girl). The environmental knowledge that she continues to carry with her and tries to pass on to us is several generations old. Instead, it is devalued and ignored, as we have been told to do. My generation has been encouraged to learn everything from 'out there' but nothing about our own traditional knowledge. Who would dare to quote our great-grandparents as a reference in graduate school? To cite from the World Bank Annual Report is much more sophisticated and secure, in terms of 'accepted' knowledge.

Looking back to the relationship between my mother and myself has helped me understand what one native elder has said about racism:

> If you truly want to conquer a people, you withdraw, but you leave your education system behind, and you won't have to do anything to them. By using the tool, the very

important and powerful tool they left behind, you'll do it to yourself (Osennontion and Skonaganleh: rá, 1989: 12).

However, in Environmental Studies at York University, I found that in most courses I could not adequately and critically participate in discussions without at some time evoking the perspective of my mother's knowledge. For example, during the session on 'Nature Toys' in 'Environmental Education through Natural Folklore', I was not familiar with, nor could I make any toys from materials indigenous to Canada. I phoned home and my mother mailed her coconut leaf toys all the way from Bangkok for display to Canadian students in Toronto. When I searched for information for my research on 'The Mayan's and My Mother's Kitchen Garden: A Political, Socio-Economic and Ecological Perspective', my mother recounted the number of different kinds of plants, herbs, flowers, spices, etc., she has in her garden. In all, there are around 90 species. Additionally, I explored the topic of the 'Environmental Politics of Paper' by investigating the relation between women and the various uses of trees, e.g. toilet tissues, napkins, paper towels and nappies, as paper consumption is often used as an index of 'wealth'. I found that the current per capita consumption rate in the US is 311 kilograms per annum, whereas over half of all African nations use less than one kilogram per capita annually (WEN, 1991: 32). It seems that my Thai mother consumes paper at a rate similar to those in these particular African nations. Above all, she never used disposable nappies in her life. Instead, she used sustainable cotton with all six of her children.

In conclusion, what I have learned most from the process of interviewing my mother includes two important aspects: *the realisation of how I myself had been colonised, and a discovery of the history that had been marginalised by mainstream development and environmental experts. The realisation of both has led me to begin the process of decolonising myself.* I confidently and proudly told

140

myself that it was not the beautiful booklets I had received in the Environmental Education class but my mother who provided a meaningful Environmental Education curriculum for me. She has been the source from which I learned how to live with, listen to and make observations on my social and natural environment. She knows many things that I don't know and cannot find in school. There are many aspects of her knowledge that are still mysteries for me. I don't know much about her and her knowledge as I had left her to join the mainstream educational system at the age of five.

Sitting on her lap, I started learning how to read and write, how to spell and count, and heard her recite many traditional lullabies, poems and folklore (of course, many of which were about different kinds of animals and plants, as well as an emphasis on human relations with nature through observing, reflecting and mimicking). By contrast, at school, and later in university, there were many unfamiliar subjects taught, such as English, Geometry, Sociology, Anthropology, Journalism and Mass Communications. These subjects were beyond my mother's comprehension, which served only to tear us apart. In the modern world, it seems that the Western knowledge that I was taught in university was assumed to be privileged, as it was something 'progressive'. Additionally, it was assumed that since this knowledge was superior, a further step towards success would be for me to go abroad and bring more advanced knowledge back, in order to continue to 'develop' Thailand (as my CIDA scholarship has explicitly indicated).

Having been born and raised during the peak of the development era, I had buried my Thai roots inside myself. The process of interviewing my mother has given me an opportunity to bring these roots, that I had buried, to the outside. To look at my own experiences through my mother's history can be a powerful way to critique Western development. By doing so, I have come to a similar conclusion as

Renee Long, who was also engaged in the decolonising process which required that she articulate that difficult 'in-between' place being Chinese-Canadian:

> [b]eing colonized creates this alien entity inside the same body, and thus divides the identity from within. Lani Maestro describes her experience of colonization as if 'another person has taken over my body, that kept me from speaking for a long time'. I am discovering the history that the colonizers excluded. From this discovery, I am filling in the missing pieces and learning new definitions and directions for dialogue about difference.
>
> Now I know I can live the words that I read. The words I have read in this course are no longer one-dimensional texts. The theories and concepts describe interpretations of the conditions of the postmodern world we live in today. I have discovered the presence of my own voice and from this new beginning, I am changed forever (1993: 48, 52).

Finally, I have come to another level in understanding the concept of 'development', one that goes beyond that of the traditional paradigm of political economy – that is, the politics of identity and difference. I began to realise that 'development' is part of that *'Westernising' process of 'excluding' difference by imposing sameness (a global consumer culture or monoculture) in terms of 'naming', 'studying', 'helping' and above all 'speaking for' the 'others'*.

Bibliography

Achebe, Chinua. *No Longer At Ease*. London: Heinemann, 1960.

Aeusrivongse, Nidhi. *Mai let Wattanatham Ruam Samai*. Bangkok: Praew Publishing House, 1994.

Anzaldúa, Gloria. Introduction. *Making Face, Making Soul: Creative and Critical Perspectives by Women of Color*. Ed. Gloria Anzaldúa. San Francisco: Aunt Lute Foundation Books, 1990.

Apisuk, Chantawipa *et al, Empower 1987 Annual Report*. Bangkok: Education Means Protection of Women Engaged in Recreation, 1987.

Apisuk, Chantawipa. 'Strip Fashion Show: Prostitution's New Development'. *Women's World* 4 (1984): 37–8.

Archavanitkul, Kritaya. 'Girl Prostitution'. *Voices of Thai Women* 4 (1990): 18–20.

Bangkok Post 15 August 1990: 15.

Bannerji, Himani. 'But Who Speaks for Us: Experience and Agency in Conventional Feminist Paradigms'. *Unsettling Relations: The University as a Site of Feminist Struggles*. Himani Bannerji *et al*. Toronto: Women's Press, 1991, 67–107.

Charoensin-o-larn, Chairat. *Understanding Postwar Reformism in Thailand*. Bangkok: Editions Duang Kamol, 1988.

Ekachai, Sanitsuda. *Behind the Smile: Voices of Thailand*. Bangkok: Thai Development Support Committee, 1990a.

— 'Slaves of the Modern World'. *Voices of Thai Women* 4 (1990b): 21–6.

Enloe, Cynthia. *Bananas, Beaches and Bases*. London: Pandora Press, 1989.

Erlanger, Steven. 'A Plague Awaits'. *The New York Times Magazine* 14 July 1991, Sec. 6: 24, 26, 49, 53.

Foundation for Women (FFW). *GATTW Newsletter* (1990): 1–4.

Gabriel-Luzon, Jo. 'Paradise and Prostitution'. *Women's World* 13 (1987): 2.

Gender and Development Research Institute (GDRI). *Information on Status and Role of Thai Women and Men*. Bangkok: GDRI, 1991.

Goulet, Denis. '"Development"… or Liberation'. *The Political Economy of Underdevelopment*. Ed. Charles K. Wilber. 2nd ed. New York: Random House, 1979, 379–86.

Griffin, Keith. *Alternative Strategies for Economic Development*. London: Macmillan, 1989.

Hantrakul, Sukanya. 'Prostitution in Thailand'. *Development and Displacement: Women in Southeast Asia*. Ed. Glen Chandler, Norma Sullivan and Jan Branson. Clayton, Vic: Centre for Southeast Asian Studies, Monash University, 1988, 115–35.

hooks, bell. *Feminist Theory: From Margin to Center*. Boston: South End Press, 1984.

Joe, Rita. 'The Gentle War'. *Canadian Women Studies*, 10. 2–3. (1989): 279.

Lewis, Arthur W. *The Theory of Economic Growth*. London: Allen and Unwin, 1955.

Long, Renee. 'Becoming Leung Mu-Yi'. *Harbour* 2.2 (1993): 47–52.

Lycklama à Nijeholt, Geertje. *Women and the Meaning of*

Development: Approaches and Consequences: Working Paper Sub-Series on Women's History and Development – No. 15. The Hague: Institute of Social Studies, 1992.

Maclean's 25 March 1991: 24.

Mies, Maria. 'Consumption Patterns of the North – the Cause of Environmental Destruction and Poverty in the South'. Paper Presented at the Symposium 'Women and Children First'. 27–30 May, 1991. Geneva: UNWED, 1991.

— *Patriarchy and Accumulation on a World Scale.* 3rd ed. London: Zed Books, 1989.

National Commission on Women's Affairs (NCWA), the Prime Minister's Office Bangkok, Thailand. Documentation of Seminar on 'The Role of Government and Private Sector in Preventing and Correcting the Sex Service Business'. 18–19 September 1990.

Nelson, Joyce. *Sultans of Sleaze: Public Relations and Media.* Toronto: Between the Lines, 1989.

Now 10–16 February 1994: 13.

O'Malley, Sean. 'Our Man in Manila'. *Saturday Night* 106 (1991): 40–45; 84–90.

Osennonion and Skonaganleh rá: 'Our World.' *Canadian Women Studies* 10. 23 (1989): 7–19.

Phongpaichit, Pasuk. *From Peasant Girls to Bangkok Masseuses.* Geneva: International Labour Office, 1982.

Ramitanondh, Shalardchai. 'Forests and Deforestation in Thailand: a Pandisciplinary Approach'. *Culture and Environment in Thailand.* Bangkok: Siam Society, 1989.

Rhodes, Richard. 'Death in the Candy Store'. *Rolling Stone* 28 November 1991: 62–114.

Ritcher, Linda K. *The Politics of Tourism.* Honolulu: University of Hawaii Press, 1989.

Schmetzer, Uli. 'In the Modern-Day Siam, Cheating is the King'. *Chicago Tribune* 13 December 1990, Sec.1:8.

Sen, Gita and Caren Grown. *Development, Crises, and Alternative Visions: Third World Women's Perspectives.* New York:

Monthly Review Press, 1987.

Shiva, Vandana. *Staying Alive: Women, Ecology and Development*. 3rd ed. London: Zed Books, 1990.

Sitthiraksa, Sinith. 'My Mother: An Unwritten Environmental Education Curriculum'. *Undercurrents* 5 (1993): 22–26.

Skrobanek, Siriporn. 'Child Prostitution in Thailand'. *Voices of Thai Women* 4 (1990a): 10–17.

— 'Tourism and the Price Women Pay'. *Voices of Thai Women* 3 (1990b): 10–13.

—'The Norwegian Women's Victory: The Court Case in Tonsberg'. *Voices of Thai Women* 3 (1990c): 14–18.

Staniland, Martin. *What is Political Economy?* New Haven and London: Yale University Press, 1985.

Streeten, Paul *et al. First Things First: Meeting Basic Human Needs in Developing Countries*. New York: Oxford University Press, 1981.

Sutherland, Ann. 'Basic Needs Consolidation Assignment': A Term Paper for ES 6168: *Basic Needs: Philosophy, Ethics and Politics*. Faculty of Environmental Studies, York University. 26 April 1993.

Suzuki, David. 'The buzz saw of "progress" hits Sarawak'. *Saturday Star* 12 March 1994.

Tantiwiramanond, Darunee and Shashi Ranjan Pandey. *By Women, For Women: A Study of Women's Organisations in Thailand*. Pasir Panjang, Singapore: Institute of Asian Studies, 1991.

The Nation 18 April 1989.

The New York Times 25 March 1991.

The Toronto Star November 1991: A1, A8.

Trainer, Ted. *Developed to Death: Rethinking Third World Development*. London: Greenprint, 1989.

Trinh, Minh-ha T. *Women, Native, Other*. Bloomington and Indianapolis: Indiana University Press, 1989.

— *Framer Framed*. New York: Routledge, 1992.

Verhelst, Thierry G. *No Life Without Roots: Culture and Develop-*

ment. Trans. Bob Cumming. London and New Jersey: Zed Books, 1990.

Women in Development Consortium in Thailand (WIDCIT). Bangkok: Thammasat University, 1989.

Wilber, Charles K. and Kenneth P. Jameson. 'Paradigms of Economic Development and Beyond'. *The Political Economy of Development and Underdevelopment*. Ed. Charles K. Wilber. 4th ed. New York: Random House, 1988, 3–27.

Women's Environmental Network (WEN). *A Tissue of Lies? Disposable Paper and the Environment*. London: WEN, 1991.

Index

BOOKS FROM ZED ON
WOMEN, THE ENVIRONMENT AND DEVELOPMENT

The Women, Gender and Development
Reader
*Edited by Nalini Visvanathan with Lynn
Duggan, Laurie Nisonoff and Nan
Wiegersma*

Staying Alive: Women, Ecology and
Development
Vandana Shiva

Women, the Environment &
Sustainable Development:
Towards a Theoretical Synthesis
*Rosi Braidotti, Ewa Charkiewicz, Sabine
Hausler and Saskia Wieringa*

Getting Institutions Right for Women in
Development
Edited by Anne-Marie Goetz

Feminist Perspectives on Sustainable
Development
Edited by Wendy Harcourt

The Elusive Agenda:
Mainstreaming Women in Development
Rounaq Jahan

Making Women Matter:
The Role of the United Nations
Hilkka Pietila and Jeanne Vickers

Ecofeminism
Maria Mies and Vandana Shiva

Gender, Education and Development
*Edited by Christine Heward and Sheila
Bunwaree*

Third World Second Sex
Edited by Miranda Davies

The Power to Change:
Women in the Third World Redefine
their Environment
Women's Feature Service

African Women and Development:
A History
Margaret M Snyder and Mary Tadesse

Gender and Development in the Arab
World: Women's Economic
Participation: Patterns and Policies
*Edited by Nabil F Khoury and Valentine M
Moghadam*

Biopolitics:
A Feminist and Ecological Reader
*Edited by Vandana Shiva and
Ingunn Moser*

Women and the Environment
*Prepared by Annabel Rodda
Women and World Development Series*

Ecofeminism as Politics:
Nature, Marx and the Postmodern
Ariel Salleh

These books should be available from all good bookshops. In case of
difficulty, please contact us:
Zed Books Ltd, 7 Cynthia St, London N1 9JF, UK.
Tel +44(0)171 837 4014; Fax +44(0)171 833 3960
e-mail: sales@zedbooks.demon.co.uk